T2-CRY-248

A Weary World

Find digital resources for study, worship, and sharing at
www.wjkbooks.com/AWearyWorld

A Weary World

Reflections for a Blue Christmas

KATHY ESCOBAR

WESTMINSTER
JOHN KNOX PRESS
LOUISVILLE · KENTUCKY

© 2020 Kathy Escobar

First Edition
Published by Westminster John Knox Press
Louisville, Kentucky

20 21 22 23 24 25 26 27 28 29—10 9 8 7 6 5 4 3 2 1

All rights reserved. No part of this book may be reproduced or transmitted in any form or by any means, electronic or mechanical, including photocopying, recording, or by any information storage or retrieval system, without permission in writing from the publisher. For information, address Westminster John Knox Press, 100 Witherspoon Street, Louisville, Kentucky 40202-1396. Or contact us online at www.wjkbooks.com.

Unless otherwise indicated, Scripture quotations are from the New Revised Standard Version of the Bible, copyright © 1989 by the Division of Christian Education of the National Council of the Churches of Christ in the U.S.A., and are used by permission. Scripture quotations marked NIV are from *The Holy Bible, New International Version*. Copyright © 1973, 1978, 1984, 2011 by Biblica, Inc.® Used by permission. All rights reserved worldwide. Scripture quotations marked NLT are taken from the Holy Bible, New Living Translation, copyright 1996, 2004. Used by permission of Tyndale House Publishers, Inc., Wheaton, Illinois 60189. All rights reserved.

Excerpt from "A Blessing in the Anger" from *The Cure for Sorrow*, by Jan Richardson, is used by permission.

Excerpt from "Be Here Now," words and music by Heather Lyn Hamilton-Chronis, © 2019 ASCAP Heatherlyn Music. Used by permission. All rights reserved.

Unimportant People Cartoon, by David Hayward, DavidHayward@nakedpastor .com. Used by permission.

Book design by Drew Stevens
Cover design by Allison Taylor

Library of Congress Cataloging-in-Publication Data is on file at the Library of Congress, Washington, DC.

ISBN: 978-0-664-26693-6

Most Westminster John Knox Press books are available at special quantity discounts when purchased in bulk by corporations, organizations, and special-interest groups. For more information, please e-mail SpecialSales@wjkbooks .com.

Contents

Introduction

The soul wants truth, not trivia.
— Parker Palmer[1]

This past Christmas was the very first Christmas I had ever dreaded. Tragically losing our son, a thriving college sophomore, to suicide with zero warning signs just shy of his twentieth birthday last year inflicted a brutal blow not only to my heart and soul but to so many people connected to our family. My husband, Jose, and our other four young adult children crawled our way through the holidays with bleeding hearts and broken souls. Even though for many years I have been writing about Christmas being hard, creating spaces to honor people's struggles during the holidays, I had never felt them myself in such a deep and profound way.

It was hard to breathe.

Everything just felt wrong, harsh, raw.

The songs felt ridiculous. The shine was off everything. The only emotion I could feel was a pervading sadness and deep empathy for every person in The Refuge—the faith community I cofounded and copastor in Colorado—who struggles with this season over the years. Sure, before our son's suicide, I had compassion and tried to be a good friend, holding other people's pain. Real-time empathy and feeling all the feelings for myself was a whole different story.

I joined a club of battered and bruised souls in a way I never expected. My husband, one of the most optimistic and forward-looking people I have ever met, joined us, too. How could we make it through Christmas with this gaping hole in our hearts? What could we do with all these conflicting feelings surrounding the holidays while we could barely breathe, and our other four young adult kids still needed us? What was possible for us to do, and what did we know was completely *impossible*?

As dreaded as those days from Thanksgiving to Christmas felt, I knew I was far from alone. Our numbers are legion. There are so many of us who—for all kinds of reasons—suffer this time of year and keep longing for hope, connection, and peace in the middle of loss, chaos, and confusion; who feel the magnitude of our weary world weighing on our hearts and souls; who are wrestling with chronic pain, broken relationships, shattered dreams, fragile faith, and unexpected losses. My friend Father Scott, a former Catholic priest and Celtic theologian, says that the Advent season is a magnifier for everyone, but in different ways. For some, *it magnifies the good, the happy, the joy. For others, it can magnify the hard, the pain, the darkness.*

This book isn't to magnify the hard, pain, and darkness—or the good, happy, and joy.

It's about honoring our weary hearts in a weary season in a weary world and traveling the road of Advent together as honestly as we can on a quest for encouragement, hope, and strength in the places we are currently living—emotionally, spiritually, and physically.

Many of us have multifaceted pain related to the season of Advent. Whether you grew up in church and observed this season of four weeks before Christmas or you have no idea what "Advent" even means, most of us have one human thing in common—*the holidays stir up both overt and often unspoken troubles.* This time of year taps into very real and present pain, usually centered on dysfunctional family wounds, painful life experiences, and brutal losses—deaths of people we loved as well as losing jobs, health, marriages, church and faith as we once knew it, and countless dreams. Add to it the sting of financial pressures, strained relationships, social distancing, pandemic disease, injustices everywhere we look, and wondering what we even believe about the Christmas story anymore, and Advent can be a very dangerous season for not only aching hearts but numb hearts as well. A lot of us are just . . . weary.

We all cope in different ways. Some put on as happy a face as we can muster, buckle in for the month, show up every Sunday morning for church, and gut it out until Christmas is over; there's a lot of teeth-grinding and white-knuckling this season. Others build a wall of protection around our hearts and survive through anger, busyness, or keeping our head down and working harder—missing church intentionally or choosing to withdraw from it altogether. Others completely fall apart and enter into a run of heightened anxiety or depression, finding relief in unhealthy ways like overeating, abusing drugs or alcohol, overspending, or overworking. For some of us, after experiencing a disorienting faith shift where much of what we used to believe fell apart, hearing the Christmas story over and over triggers a fresh level of pain, disconnection, and unbelief. When we've joined the ranks of the nones, dones, or spiritual but not religious, or maybe consider ourselves agnostic or atheist—we see the hypocrisy of forced belief and the rituals that maybe used to bring us comfort. A lot of us are on the outside of the religious circles we once called home.

No matter what our circumstances are—practical or faith-based—I want to honor that this time of year can be extra hard, extra weird, and extra lonely.

This season can remind us of some painful things:

— *We've suffered losses*: people, jobs, dreams, health, faith, church communities where we were once members. Our losses are magnified this time of year.

— *We aren't where we wish we were in our lives.* We don't have money, partners, children, health, security, friends, community, healing, sobriety, or a host of other things we thought we would, and our disappointment is more illuminated.

— *We are worn down and weary.* The current political and religious climate has felt exhausting for so many, the grind of division between our family and friends, a never-ending news cycle. Real life also takes its toll; often, families are struggling, kids are taxing, jobs are stressful, churches are unfulfilling. We're exhausted and want to skip over December or crawl under the covers and not reemerge until mid-January.

— *We feel alone.* Some of us feel lonely in the relationships we are in, while others feel lonely because we don't have them at all.

— *We are in the middle of crises.* Unexpected personal and professional chaos, finding our way through pandemics, and significant life changes have left us depleted and disoriented.

— *Our families are nonexistent or tricky* (you might have other words for it). While some families are easier than others, often the forced connection dredges up feelings of anxiety and dread. For many, there's no home to go to; we are painfully reminded of being orphaned or the harsh realities of divorce and single parenthood.

— *We feel disconnected and confused in our faith.* We might not have a church or community that feeds us like before or even feels safe enough to enter. Our old spiritual tricks don't work anymore, and we just aren't sure what we believe these days.

— *We don't do well with inauthenticity in this season of our story.* The forced parties, buying gifts that people don't need, and a host of other cultural expectations for family and friends and work feels fake, and we don't have the energy to pull it off.

— *We are scared of hope.* The Advent season is supposed to be a time of hope and anticipation; yet, for a lot of us, hope feels far too dangerous. Hope makes us vulnerable, and we don't want to let our guard down or get hurt again.

You probably have some other ones to add as well. If you're in any of these places right now, I hope that picking up this book somehow makes you feel less alone. We are in good company this blue Christmas. We're not crazy. We're not faithless. We're not weak.

We're just human.

Being honest about our humanity is always better than hiding.

This journey we are about to take together through Advent could be the right place for you for this season. However, I want to start with a disclaimer: if you are feeling extremely happy, connected, and joyful right now, I am warning you that I'm not sure a lot of these words will resonate. That's okay. There are countless Advent devotionals available that might offer a better fit for you.

My intent for this book is to create a space for people who just aren't feeling like singing "Joy to the World" right now, who are holding on to our faith by a thread, who are grieving and crawling our way through pain and loss in a myriad of ways, who are longing for hope and peace and know that trite words won't get us there. It's for people who want to engage with their own story, the Christmas story, and the world's story in a way that feels honest, raw, and vulnerable. It's for groups that want to create greater connection and intimacy and avoid the spiritual platitudes and surface conversations that pervade so many church circles, especially this time of year.

Yet, while this journey together will be raw and honest, I also believe it is filled with hope. Hope comes from embracing paradox and contradicting things living in the same space at the same time. It comes from real stories. It comes from engaging with the stories in the Bible with a new lens that shatters the veneer of a false positivity built on "just believing the right things."

This book is divided into four sections with daily reflections for the four weeks of Advent, but you can pace yourself however you need. These major themes are honoring reality, practicing honesty, embracing paradox, and borrowing hope. Each of the themes are -ing words for a reason. They are actions of the soul, meant to be practiced. Owning our current story, sharing real feelings, holding paradoxical things in tension, and borrowing hope to keep on keeping on are not simple, but possible. We'll use some passages from the Christian lectionary and other wisdom teachers mixed in with stories and reflections that we'll all connect to in different ways. There will also be a place for personal reflection, prayer and journaling prompts, group discussion questions, and practices to consider trying. At the end of the book are some resources for ministry leaders and for people who aren't necessarily struggling with Christmas but want to be good friends to those who are, as well as ideas for creating Blue Christmas gatherings. Online, you'll find even more resources to help you and your church or group of friends to acknowledge and support one another in the challenges of this season. Visit www.wjkbooks.com/AWearyWorld for social media shareables and other web-ready elements for gatherings that may have moved online due to social distancing requirements.

I hope you will use all this material in any way that works for you. That might be reading this book alone or in a group or as a faith community. It might be using this content to create various Blue Christmas experiences and conversations in your group or church, either online or in real life. It might be reading a reflection each day or catching up at the end of the week. Some of the reflections will likely resonate more than others, but what I hope for overall is that *your heart and soul will feel a little relief*—that in the middle of whatever Advent angst you're experiencing, you'd feel a bit of the burden lifted and a greater sense of being in good company with other weary travelers as well.

Many churches sing "O Holy Night" on Christmas Eve. The most well-known stanza is this:

> O holy night, the stars are brightly shining,
> It is the night of the dear Saviour's birth.
> Long lay the world in sin and error pining,
> 'Till he appeared and the soul felt its worth.
> A thrill of hope the weary world rejoices,
> For yonder breaks a new and glorious morn;
> Fall on your knees, Oh hear the angel voices!
> O night divine! O night when Christ was born.[2]

For those of us who are experiencing a season that's blue, we're not quite ready for rejoicing, shining stars, glorious mornings. We hope they'll come, but right now the words "weary world" are what resonates. We're weary. We're angsty. We're falling on our knees because we're crawling, not rejoicing.

I'm crawling right along with you, and like all things in life here on earth, we're always better together.

That's really what *A Weary World: Reflections for a Blue Christmas* is about: crawling our way toward Christmas together.

As we begin, let's take a deep breath.

Let our tears fall.

Honor exactly where we are today—the good, the bad, the ugly, the beautiful.

Give our hearts permission to feel what they need to feel.

Open ourselves up to healing.

Listen for God's gentle whispers.

Take good care of ourselves.

Keep crawling toward the light together.

Let our weary souls feel a little less alone.

WEEK ONE

Honoring Reality

Sunday
Introduction

Our brokenness is always lived and experienced as highly personal, intimate and unique. I am deeply convinced that each human being suffers in a way no other human being suffers.
— Henri Nouwen[1]

The Refuge community I copastor is one of the most honest places I've ever experienced. People tell it like it is. They aren't afraid to share real problems, real pain. For some, it's refreshing; it's nice to hear the human experience expressed freely and fully. For others, it's extremely uncomfortable. Sometimes it's a combination of both. Hearing out loud some of the things swirling around in people's heads and hearts can be rattling. We're not used to so much raw and real.

I think it's what we (and especially the church) all need to get more comfortable with—*raw and real.*

The human experience is filled with struggle and strife. It's filled with anxiety, fear, shame, and doubt. Yet at the same time, it's also filled with hope, love, and faith. Our real stories don't discount the good, and we don't need to put a "but" at the end of each challenging thing we share to somehow minimize the pain. I do it, too. It's hard to just say, "I am suffering" without adding "but I'm still getting up every day" or "but I've got a lot to be thankful for," or all kinds of words that soften it.

Honoring reality is healthy.

There are so many troublesome things in the world right now, so many tricky things in most all our lives. Even if we're not directly experiencing a lot of emotional pain, we almost certainly know someone who is. The coronavirus pandemic, which at the time I'm writing this is wreaking havoc globally, is causing life as we knew it to grind to a halt, and we have no idea what will happen next. People across the street and around the globe are now experiencing a new kind of shared societal pain.

Many of us hold pain from the loss of people, relationships, dreams. We're experiencing trauma and health issues and are deeply distraught about the state of the world related to politics and religion, climate change and the destruction of the planet, racial injustice, and the ravages of inequality. We're often feeling a paralyzing sense of helplessness about how we can be part of the change we want to see in the world—or we are so tired of fighting our own battles that we don't have what we need to advocate for others in a healthy way.

The list of painful realities is different and unique for each of us. As I quoted Henri Nouwen at the beginning of this chapter, "Each human being suffers in a way no other human suffers."[2] We have to be careful not to compare our suffering to others', thinking ours isn't valid enough, or on the other hand, believing ours is the worst pain ever, such that no one could possibly understand how we feel.

Honoring our own unique realities is just that—*honoring our unique realities*. It's owning that no matter what we're feeling or experiencing related to life and faith, it's our story. It's the place we need healing, hope, connection. For some of us, we're feeling the need for God.

I want to be tender and careful when it comes to talking about God here because we're probably all over the place in how we're experiencing God these days and where we are on our own distinctive faith journeys—yet you need to know where I'm coming from, too. This is an Advent book, and I do still believe in the work of God in the world, in my life, in the lives of others, and in the ways of Jesus, which always lead downward into the problems and pain of real life. At this stage of my life, I've shed much rigid and damaging theology, and my faith has been stripped down to a place where there's so much I really don't know and don't try to know anymore that some people might wonder if anything's even left. What remains seems to be all I need, and I am finding that it's sustaining us through our darkest night.

I have had one simple truth remain—*Emmanuel, God with us*. It's a prevailing belief that somehow, someway, God is indeed with us in the muck and mire of our current realities—with us, alongside us, in, around, through, above, and below us. Jesus, God in the flesh, embodying the way of Love from which we can learn. For some of you, that's comforting, and others of you might feel yourself scoffing.

I get it. Often, that's just reality.

For me, it's enough.

My desire isn't that you believe a certain way or even believe at all. There's room for all of us here. My only hope is that you focus this week on honoring your own unique and personal reality; on tenderly holding your story and seeing yourself in others' stories as well; on acknowledging our shared humanity, letting go of trying to figure things out, and opening yourself up to some tenderness.

Advent is about waiting. It's about expectation. It's about anticipating the birth of Jesus—and in a lot of our churches we were taught that Jesus alone would solve all our problems. Some of you can't buy that anymore. You've seen too much life, experienced too much hardship, crawled through too many dark nights of the soul, and you can't take anything that smells of dishonesty, insincerity, or quick fixes.

I am right there with you. Long before my son died, I had some of the same feelings. The neat and tidy Christmas story that's often presented to us just didn't work for me, and still doesn't.

We've sanitized a messy, weird, and upside-down story, and it's done us all a disservice. Regardless of whether right now God feels near and tender or far and distant from you, that's where we're going to dive in this week—the human reality of our current stories and the human reality of the Christmas story, too.

The Scripture read in many churches this first week of Advent is Mark 13:24–37. You can read it on your own if you want to, but my favorite line is the very last: "Keep awake" (v. 37).

For some, you're agonizingly awake to your story right now. It's keeping you up at night, doing a number on your head and heart. For others, we're trying to tune it out, numb it out, do whatever we can to not feel it.

Wherever you are, I honor you. It makes me think of the words of grief therapist and writer Francis Weller: "To be human is to know loss in its many forms. Rather than hearing this as a depressing truth, our ability to acknowledge this reality enables us to find our way into the grace that lies hidden in sorrow. We are most alive at the threshold between loss and revelation; every loss ultimately opens the way for a new encounter."[3]

This week we're going to do what we can to open the way for a new encounter, dive in together, awaken to what's going on in our weary souls, consider the Jesus story more honestly, and honor our present reality together.

What's your current reality? What's going on in your life that's making your soul weary? What's missing that you long for?

Monday
The Real Christmas Story

We bless the messy wonder of it all,
the experience of being human.

—Mirabai Starr[4]

A lot of us have a profound conflict in our hearts about Christmas. How we celebrate Christmas, tell the stories of Christmas, and the façades that are put on in church and in the world just do not seem right.

This rumbling in our souls is worth listening to.

Human beings like a cleaner, neater story, theologies that fit into a box, and easy answers to complicated questions. We like staying in our comfort zones, boundaries to keep out the riff-raff and help us maintain life on our terms. For the most part, humans like formulas: *if I do this, believe this, act like this, then* _____ *will happen.*

But we've all been around long enough to know that is *not* real life.

The real Christmas story isn't clean, neat, or tidy. It's a crazy, wild story: God, choosing to reveal himself in a human baby born to unwed parents in a dirty stall filled with animals and chaos. The least likely people are the ones drawn to him while royalty wants to kill him. The images we often see of the Nativity look perfect and serene, with an adoring Mary gazing at Jesus while the animals watched.

Reality: It was a smelly, noisy, bloody, and painful scene. *Smelly, noisy, bloody, and painful.*

Kind of like a lot of our lives are right now, too.

I have no idea where you are specifically, but I know my story right now is smelly, noisy (in my head), bloody, and excruciatingly painful. Each day is a stretch to make it through, and in the midst of all our pain is the pain of so many others in my circle—losses, deaths, addictions, mental illnesses, despair, pandemic concerns, identity crises, homelessness, loneliness. It's a lot to hold—and we live in suburban comfort. The thought of a neat and tidy God is not only *not comforting*; it makes me want to run the other direction.

But the thought of Jesus as a human being all tangled up in the mess of real life and all of the dynamics of pain, suffering, confusion, shame, exhaustion, and perseverance in the midst of these things—that's a story that draws me in.

What's smelly, noisy, bloody, and painful in your life right now?

Tuesday
The Unimportant People

It's hard to be human. A lot of us were taught in our church stories that part of our work is to become more like God. They forget that God's big revelation in the Christmas story is becoming *more human*. While my faith has changed drastically over the years and I have shed so many theological constructs and spiritual practices I once held dear, I have remained rooted in the Christian story for this exact reason.

God came into the world as a human.

God is with us in our humanity.

The stories in Scripture that flesh out Jesus' arrival couldn't point to this more clearly.

God, a human being, in all the mess and blood and guts of birth. Parents, unwelcomed in all the places they tried to find rest and shelter. A wailing baby boy, born to nobodies with animals bleating all around. Lowly shepherd kids, the first to know. Unlikely pagan astrologers strangely drawn to come and see this special baby.

Over and over again, we see the important people — the people who have things all figured out, the religiously certain, the ones who hold power — with hardened hearts and who fear doing anything that would make them lose their position.

Today, all these years later, the same story is unfolding.

The "important" people are often actively trying to stay separated from others, to remain protected in homogeneous Christian bubbles, working to exclude, protect, hunker down, and make sure they stay comfortable and safe. Meanwhile, the messy, the hurting, the desperate, and the marginalized are sloshing around in the beautiful mess of the upside-down ways of Jesus and illuminating the first line in his Sermon on the Mount — "Blessed are the poor in spirit, for theirs is the kingdom of heaven" (Matthew 5:3).

The Christmas story reminds us that the unimportant people were always at the center of it all. The story was always about turning power on its head; about hope for the unimportant, the humble, open, desperate, and willing; about flesh and blood, mess and glory, pain and suffering, hope and beauty, mercy and weirdness and how love was and is being born again and again and again in all the unimportant people.

Jesus' profound truth about the reign of God continues to rise to the surface against all odds — "The last will be first and the first will be last" (Matthew 20:16).

If you're on the fringes, feel like you don't belong, and can't seem to catch a break — remember this truth, remember this image, and remember you're in good company.

Spend a few minutes reflecting on the above Nativity cartoon by my friend David Hayward. What does it stir up in you today?

Wednesday
Weary

The air was thick with stories.

—Ruth Hogan[5]

In my life pastoring The Refuge community and connecting with other people in real life and online from around the world, I get to hear so many important stories. It's a gift I treasure. But it's also intense, too, with the air being so thick with real stories. Just this week I talked to single moms struggling to keep the lights on, people living in their cars trying everything they know to secure affordable housing, disabled veterans trying to manage their posttraumatic stress disorder (PTSD), burned-out pastors straining to find a new vocation, friends in the middle of divorces and raising kids in this crazy world, and survivors of religious trauma who long for a freer connection with God. In this season of my story navigating the deepest grief, I cry every day.

Every single day.

Every. Single. Day.

Waves of grief are part of my current story, and I can do nothing about them except ride them out. One after another after another. It's exhausting.

When you think of the word *weary*, what comes to mind? For me, it's *tired, exhausted, out of steam, depleted, worn-out, longing for relief.*

So many people seem extra weary this time of year.

My friends are weary.

I'm weary.

The world is weary.

Political strife, amplified division, relational struggles, world crises, the onslaught of social media and a culture where smartphone notifications often control us can make us tired. Even if we try to tune out the outside rumble, our own struggles often wear us down.

Then we hear all kinds of messages about taking time for ourselves so that we're not so tired—to slow down, rest, find a way toward peace. These notions are all good, and I am a passionate advocate for soul care that helps us last. Remember that it's a privilege to have the space and time for the kind of self-care we wish were possible for everyone, and many of us don't have those resources. I believe everyone can find ways to find some kind of relief, no matter how small or insignificant it might seem, but we also need to honor that sometimes when we're struggling to keep our heads above water, to just survive, the best we can do is keep breathing: one breath and then the next. Today, I also think it's good to remember that sometimes no matter what we do to rest and take good care of our souls, sometimes at the end of the day, we're still just . . . weary.

The air is thick with stories.
We live in a weary world.
Rejoicing sometimes has to wait.

What's making you extra weary today?

Thursday
Let It Be

In times of trouble, Mother Mary comes to me,
Speaking words of wisdom, let it be.
—John Lennon and Paul McCartney[6]

This past Christmas Eve as I was preparing for The Refuge service, I was overwhelmed with the reality of our first Christmas without our son. How could this be real? How could we now be a family of six and not seven? How could I have given birth to that kid, nursed him, raised him, launched him into the world, and now he was gone? Shock waves reverberate through my body every time I realize, yet again, the magnitude of our loss.

I couldn't get Mary out of my head.

No matter what you believe about the Nativity story, Mary, the mother of Jesus, is the symbol of a mother throughout the world. An icon. A saint. A young girl whose entire life was turned upside down in an instant. An unlikely woman tasked with giving birth to Jesus in a mucky, dirty stable in Palestine. A grown mother who watched her son suffer and die before her very eyes three decades later.

Mother Mary knew trouble.

I have no doubt she also knew feelings of shame, fear, doubt, confusion, and pain. She had to move forward despite so many obstacles and countless unknowns, yet she would do anything for the child who grew inside of her. She would find a way to walk the path set before her, even when she had no idea where exactly it was going to lead.

Mothers are amazing like that.

I also love that there's a lot more to mother in this world than human beings, and that all of us—across gender—can mother and be mothered.

All of us can mother grief, beauty, dreams, pain, justice, mercy, hope, and wisdom into this troubled world.

And we can be mothered — by God in all God's wisdom, presence, strength, hope, and mercy; by the people in our lives; by music and nature and art; by Mother Mary, standing right in front of us, speaking words of wisdom like, "Let it be."

Do you need to hear that today?

Let it be.

Let it be.

Let it be.

I don't know what your soul feels specifically today, but my guess is that most of us could use a little more mothering. We need comfort, love, wisdom, hope.

If those words are for you, too, I hope you will hear their whisper: *Let it be.*

What do you need to "let be" today?

Friday
"I Don't Know"

Some things cannot be fixed. They can only be carried.
—Megan Devine[7]

There is a phrase I say a lot that I am intentionally trying to remove from my vocabulary: "I need to just figure it out." I am not saying that sometimes there aren't a lot of problems to solve or we don't need to apply critical thinking skills to particular situations, but the reality is that most times I say these words—"I need to just figure it out"—I am trying to use my brain to solve matters of the soul. I am attempting to find a shortcut out of pain, complicated situations, or heart realities that truly aren't "figure-out-able."

Believing I can always figure it out most often only leads to exhaustion, shame, and frustration. It's been one of the hardest things for me and my husband related to Jared's death; with no clues, no signs, no indicators in any of his relationships or communications, our human brains keep grasping for any and all possibilities to make sense of it. Jared loved philosophy and had a tattoo on his leg that said, "I don't know," adapted from words often attributed to Aristotle: "The more you know, the more you know you don't know." After he died, my husband, Jose—who always said he'd never get a tattoo—felt compelled to get the same one on his leg: "I don't know." I am unbelievably thankful for that tattoo because it is a tangible reminder that every time we try to figure it out, we circle back to the same landing: *I don't know.*

Living with the tension of things not being figure-out-able is usually a foreign task for humans addicted to knowing. Honoring pain, not trying to find a quick bypass to an easier path, and not numbing out are tricky work, but healthy work, too.

It makes me think of some of the stories that are part of Jesus' birth, and how so much of it doesn't make sense with our limited scope. Actually, I think our effort to sanitize Jesus' story is to make it fit better into our little boxes. We forget that not one thing looked like the pictures we see.

Just like the Christmas story, a lot of our struggle is that we are always trying to figure things out, to put our past and present into a box that fits, to work hard to heal and make sense of our own story, the stories of the world. It can be exhausting. Plus, it usually leads us nowhere but traveling around in a circle, spinning and overthinking.

I'm not saying we don't have a part to play in moving some things forward, but I believe in every part of my soul that some circumstances and realities can't be figured out and that "I don't know" is sometimes the best we can do.

What do you need to try to let go of trying to figure out today?

Saturday
Let's Just Be Honest . . .

I have learned things in the dark that I could never have learned in the light, things that have saved my life over and over again, so that there is really only one logical conclusion. I need darkness as much as I need light.
— Barbara Brown Taylor[8]

We made it through our first week of the season together! Whether you are traveling through this material alone or with a group, I stand in solidarity with you. Everyone has picked up *A Weary World* for different reasons, but I hope somehow you could find your reality in the story.

While honoring reality is the best place to start, it can sometimes stir up trouble for us, too. Pema Chodron, a Buddhist nun, has wisdom for us from her tradition: "When something hurts in life, we don't usually think of it as our path or as the source of wisdom. In fact, we think that the reason we're on the path is to get rid of this painful feeling. . . . At that level of wanting to get rid of our feeling, we naively cultivate a subtle aggression against ourselves."[9] We think, *If we could just feel or do such-and-so, then everything would be better.*

We also often believe that we're more messed up than other people or we dismiss our own unique reality as not as relevant as others. We minimize our seemingly ordinary pain in light of all the suffering in the world. Or we find ourselves trying to find an easier fix, a shortcut, a bypass — anything to quickly feel better. In the spirit of honoring our own particular angsty Advent, I'll say that minimizing and trying to find shortcuts are dangerous steps. Instead of owning our feelings *just as they are* — and letting that be enough — we often try to find our way out of the discomfort as fast as possible. Then we're mad, hurt, resentful, and ashamed when the feelings don't go away like we had hoped, and the painful cycle continues.

Another thing that often happens when we begin to honor our reality more directly is that others don't know quite what to do with us. Our culture isn't the best at grief, pain, and struggle, and the church tends to be even worse. Other people feel anxiety and fear around us when we're hurting and end up saying a lot of not-so-helpful things to try to cajole us into feeling better as quickly as possible. Usually, these suggestions aren't about us but more about relieving the other person's own anxiety. A lot of us don't have safe people to be brutally honest with, so we try to sort things out in our own head instead—which usually doesn't go too well. Anne Lamott says it best: "My mind is a bad neighborhood I try not to go into alone."[10]

Honoring our reality is not an easy task, but I hope we can each keep practicing it. I wish we could sit together in my living room or at The Refuge and share what's really going on right now—what we've lost, what we're wrestling with, what's hurting, and how you are making it through this season so far. Saying that this Christmas is "blue" doesn't tell the whole story; in the midst of pain and strife are all kinds of good things, too—some more evident than others.

My hope is that we can own our stories *just as they are*, and that we can find a bit of kinship with the upside-down Jesus story in the Scriptures that starts with God being born in the least likely of places. I hope we can consider letting ourselves be mothered in ways we might need—by God and others—and that we'll let what we can be and stop trying to figure everything out because some things just won't ever make sense.

As we wrap up this week, remember—no matter where you are, it's okay.

Honoring reality helps us practice greater honesty. That's where we're going next week, but first, consider trying some of the practices and group reflection questions for this first week. Honor your story. Find yourself in the big story. Listen to someone else's story.

A Prayer for
Honoring Reality

God,
Help us live in the places that don't make sense.
Help us keep hobbling through the hard.
Help us remember that no matter how confused,
    broken, tired, or faithless we might feel,
        you are with us and we are part of your story.

To Practice

1. **Light candles.**

Years ago, at a Refuge workshop, my friend facilitated an exercise where we shared what we were struggling with and lit as many candles as we needed. With each candle we lit, we said these words: "God, please help. . . ." I lit a candle for the world, for friends who were struggling with life and faith, and then I lit one last candle for me. Just for me. With each one, I prayed this simple prayer—"God help. . . ." In this same season, I made some candles for my friends as gifts with these words printed on the outside to remind them (and me): "I am loved. I am not alone. I am human. God is near." You might have some other words you'd write, but the practice is this—light as many candles as you need to *honor your reality, the people in your life's reality, and the world's reality.* Express what you need to say out loud or in some other tangible way.

2. **Create a meditation or mantra especially for this season.**

Meditations and mantras were practiced by the early church fathers and mothers for many years. Many things are beyond our control; however, we can take responsibility for our own states of mind. Meditation is a means of transforming the mind. The word for *mantra* has two parts; *man*, which is the root of the Sanskrit word for "mind," and *tra*, the root of the word "instrument." Mantras or chants are phrases packed with energy and intention designed to create healing, insight, and growth. Try this exercise to create one or more specifically for this season.

Pick a mantra from the list below or create one of your own. Each one is separated into two parts for a reason. The first part is breathing in; the part following the dash is breathing out.

I will be open to experiencing peace and love—this holiday
*   season.*
I will do what is necessary for me—to get through the holidays.
I will remember— I am connected and loved.
I am not alone—this holiday season.
I got this—even when I can't see the light.
I am open to creating—a season to remember.
I will not let anxiety or fear—control me this season.
Create your own:
_____ — _____.

You can repeat this as many times as you need. Begin with a centering breath and continue to breathe through the phrases as many times as you need.

3. **Tell someone your truth.**

Find a safe person and let that person know what's happening with you this season. Be honest. Live with the vulnerability. Honor your reality out loud instead of trying to navigate it on your own.

For Group Reflection

Consider implementing these guidelines for group discussion to make sure the group remains as safe and brave as possible. These are from my book *Practicing: Changing Yourself to Change the World* and can be adapted in any way that works best for your particular group's context:

— Stick with "I" statements and your own story.
— Maintain confidentiality.
— Go around the room for some of the questions and make space to hear from everyone instead of only hearing the loudest voices. Give everyone freedom to pass.
— Don't fix or offer unsolicited advice. Practice listening.
— Honor the time with brevity and keep your sharing to three to five minutes (or whatever time you decide depending on how many people you have in the group) to ensure that everyone has a chance to share.
— Do at least one round of hearing from everyone before opening the conversation up to additional reflections. Otherwise, you may never hear from some participants in the group.[11]

1. What's happening in your world or the wider world that's making you feel weary right now? What's your current reality?

2. Be honest about the Christmas story for you this season. What do you like about it? What parts are comforting? What is annoying or hard to embrace?

3. Consider the reflections from Week One. What resonated most with you? With what major themes, quotes, or words did you connect?

WEEK TWO

Practicing Honesty

Sunday
Introduction

Emotions are celebrated and repressed, analyzed and medicated,
adored and ignored—but rarely, if ever, are they honored.
—Karla McLaren[1]

As I mentioned last week in our focus on honoring reality, these days my husband and I cry daily. We never know when the feeling will come; we can be in the middle of a perfectly normal conversation, doing just fine in the moment, and something triggers the reality of our loss and a new onslaught of tears. A few minutes later we might be laughing at something one of our young adult kids texts us or we see on social media. It's the strangest feeling, and sometimes feels like what my friend Joanna calls *emotional whiplash*. It's hard on a nervous system—and a heart—and sure can make our souls weary. I'm guessing some of you might understand this feeling, too, where the range of your current emotions is wide and unpredictable; you never know what might emerge, when that might happen, and where you might be in the moment.

For some of us, our families, life experiences, and church stories taught us that certain emotions were acceptable while others weren't. In my family, I was praised for being happy and positive; if I expressed any negative emotions, the covert (and sometimes overt) message was that painful emotions, or those perceived as "bad," weren't acceptable. I learned to separate from my heart and do whatever I could to put on my game face. Another consequence of not developing a repertoire of honest feelings has been sometimes not even knowing what I *am* actually feeling. Does this sound familiar?

Often, we're so disconnected from what's going on inside of us or conditioned to do whatever possible to manage any negative feelings that we aren't sure how to articulate them. Many of us are used to glossing over feelings, pushing them down, or having no safe spaces to process them, so eventually the feelings come out sideways—often doing damage to ourselves and others around us. We might either tell ourselves, or hear from others, "Why dwell on the past?" Then we try to push aside or neglect significant feelings from the past that are affecting our present. For others, we've been working hard on learning how to notice in a healthier way what's really going on inside of us and are seeing some of those benefits. Regardless of our own unique circumstances, most of us need continual practice at being honest and sharing what we're really feeling—to ourselves, others, and God, too.

In the Christmas story at a surface level, Mary and Joseph are mostly portrayed as near-perfect people who don't have any negative feelings attached to their circumstances; they just do what they need to do because an angel told them to. Yet we know they were human beings with real feelings; fear, shame, confusion, and doubt all are strong possibilities in their unique circumstance. We can find evidence of some of these feelings through a deeper look at the Scriptures as well as honestly considering what most any human might feel in their circumstance. (Matthew 1:19 alone suggests immense internal torment for Joseph as he weighs his code of ethics and the likely consequences for Mary, deciding ultimately "to dismiss her quietly.")

Last week, the reflections centered on honoring reality. For the second week of Advent, we're going to engage with *practicing honesty*. What does this phrase stir up in you? I love the word *practice* for a lot of reasons. Mostly, it's that I don't think we have enough places and spaces to try to live something out in a different way. Practice is about "[participating] in an activity or implementing a skill repeatedly to develop greater proficiency."[2] In a world that almost automatically defaults to what is most comfortable, it's hard to practice honesty—to own our genuine and often uncomfortable emotions, to articulate and express them, to own our truth. When Christmas feels blue and our hearts and souls are weary, engaging with our emotions can sometimes feel like too much work. At the same time, it can be healing to acknowledge what's actually swirling around inside of us and practice honesty as best we can.

This week's Scripture passage is centered on John the Baptist, the messenger of Jesus, who comes before him. Mark 1:1–4 says,

> The beginning of the good news of Jesus Christ, the Son of God.
>   As it is written in the prophet Isaiah,
>
>> "See, I am sending my messenger ahead of you,
>>   who will prepare your way;
>> the voice of one crying out in the wilderness:
>>   'Prepare the way of the Lord, make his paths
>>   straight,'"

John the baptizer appeared in the wilderness, proclaiming a baptism of repentance for the forgiveness of sins.

Sometimes when I read certain Scriptures on particular days and times in my life, they make me cringe (can some of you relate?). At first glance, this passage didn't sit well with me because talk of sin and repentance immediately bring to mind a fire-and-brimstone sermon. However, these days I often try to practice *Lectio Divina*, the practice of reading a piece of Scripture or poem several times out loud and noticing what words or feelings emerge. If you have an allergy to the Bible because of a faith deconstruction, it can be helpful to engage without considering all the minutia about Greek translations or context and instead just tune in to what rises to the surface and stirs your soul. For me, in this passage in Mark, the words that keep resonating are this simple phrase: "the voice of one crying out in the wilderness."

Suspend all the things you know about John the Baptist at the moment and only consider that phrase—*the voice of one crying out in the wilderness.*

Now consider that maybe it's your voice (or the voice of someone else close to you) crying out in the wilderness and break it down even further.

Your voice. What's happening in your head and heart right now that is consuming you, troubling you, surprising you, inspiring you, stirring you?

Crying out. It might be tears of pain, anger, fear, shame, sadness, or grief, or maybe cries of joy or celebration. There are all kinds of cries of the heart.

In the wilderness. Maybe we're alone, lonely, feeling like we are wandering in the desert spiritually and emotionally. What is your wilderness right now?

This week we're going to walk through some emotions we might be experiencing this holiday season—anger, grief, sadness, fear, shame, and confusion. You may identify with some more strongly than others, but my hope is that we find some relief and peace knowing we're in good company in the wilderness.

What emotions are you feeling most acutely today?

Monday
Anger

Anger is a signal, and one worth listening to.
—Harriet Lerner[3]

Anger is one of the most misunderstood and underrated emotions in our culture, which is one of the reasons it often manifests in violence and destructive words. When we're taught that the real feeling of anger is *bad*, we do what humans do best—try to manage it in ways that end up being unhealthy, resulting in damage to ourselves and others and often to our relationship with God, too.

For many years, I kept my anger under wraps, but when my first two children were very young, I began sharing feelings more honestly in a women's group at our church for the very first time. Among them was deep anger at my family, myself, and God. At first, it wasn't easy for me to express it without adding "but" to each sentence. I'd say, "I'm really mad about . . . *but* God is good," ". . . *but* I have so much to be grateful for," ". . . *but* I know it's not okay to stay here for long," or a host of other *buts* that were ways of minimizing my anger to be more acceptable.

Many of us have been taught that if we had more faith, more humility, more [fill in your own blank], then we wouldn't be angry.

The truth is that anger is a healthy and real emotion and a very appropriate response to injustice and pain. In the Letter to the Ephesians, the apostle Paul writes, "Be angry but do not sin" (4:26), not "it's a sin to be angry," which is what I was always taught in church. Releasing our anger and being honest about what is making us mad are healthy actions. Right now, everyone in our lives knows I am angry at my deceased son for not reaching out to anyone and for the collateral damage of his decision. My tangible and present anger is part of my grief. It's part of my reality.

For the past eight years at The Refuge we have hosted a special contemplative gathering in early December called Blue Christmas. It is a mix of a short, shared liturgy and then an extended time with seven or eight experiential stations set up around our facility that people can engage with at their own pace. One of the most popular stations is our ornament smashing station, focused on freely expressing anger and translating that into an embodiment exercise that releases some of it in a healthy way. We take time to write what we're angry about on glass ornaments and then smash them against a wall. What happens in that space every year is amazing.

Owning our anger is extraordinarily brave.

It makes me think of this line from Jan Richardson in her book of blessings, *The Cure for Sorrow*:

> Trust
> that the other face
> of anger
> is courage,
> that it holds the key
> to your secret strength,
> that the fire it offers
> will light your way.[4]

What are you angry about right now?

Tuesday
Grief

The LORD is near to the brokenhearted.
—Psalm 34:18

The aforementioned writer and artist Jan Richardson lost her husband suddenly several years ago, giving her profound insight into and wisdom on the realities of sadness, heartbreak, and grief. While many of us were taught that grief has clear stages and part of our healing is moving through them one by one, Jan says this:

> Grief is the least linear thing I know. Hardly a tidy progression of stages, grief tends to be unruly. It works with the most raw and elemental forces in us, which makes it unpredictable and wild. Grief resists our attempts to force it along a prescribed path. It propels us in directions we had not planned to go. It causes what we treated as solid to give way. It opens new seams of mourning in places we thought settled. It spirals us back through layers of sorrow we thought we had dealt with.[5]

This description resonates deeply in my soul. Grief looks like spiraling through layers of sorrow, not just every day but often every hour.

While Jan and I unexpectedly lost people we dearly loved, many of us are experiencing deep sadness in different ways. It might be loneliness; physical, emotional, or spiritual pain; loss, disappointment; despair about injustice and oppression and our current political system; rejection from our families; or a variety of other situations. Regardless of the range of our losses, two things remain clear to me—*there's a lot of heartbreak in the world*, and *grief has no rules.*

Grief has no rules.

Jesus was well acquainted with grief and the human experience. He wept openly, sweated blood, cried out in agony. As we celebrate the incarnation of God, born into the world as a human, this season reminds us of this truth: Jesus intimately knows these feelings we're experiencing, too.

The Psalms are also filled with raw and vulnerable songs that express the cry of our human hearts. I have made several trips to Israel and Palestine over the years, and one of my favorite stops is the Western Wall in Jerusalem (often referred to as the Wailing Wall), where people from around the globe have been openly praying and weeping for generations. That wall holds a lot of pain and is a holy, thin space where heaven and earth meet. It makes me think of the Old Testament passage in Psalm 56:8 (NLT):

> You keep track of all my sorrows.
>> You have collected all my tears in your bottle.

In this weary world, a lot of tears are being shed right now, wide varieties of grief churning in people and communities near and far. It makes me wonder if the imagery of our tears comprising the oceans is somehow much more appropriate than contained in a bottle.

No matter what imagery you appreciate, consider your grief right now and know that while it can feel overwhelming, we are in good company with people from every tribe and nation—weeping, wailing, grieving, brokenhearted.

Remember, grief has no rules.

What's causing pain right now, no matter how big or small? What are you grieving? What is your heart breaking over?

Wednesday
Fear

Fear will always be there, poised and ready to wreak havoc,
but we can choose whether we're going to engage with it
or turn on the lights, drown it out and crawl past it.
— Jen Sincero[6]

Years ago, when our oldest son was getting ready to leave for college across the country, we were standing in his room talking about the transition when he broke down sobbing. I'll never forget Josh's words: "I am so scared! The truth is I just want to stay here with you guys and live in my room here forever." Practicing honesty this way wasn't easy for him, but it helped us all. We got a glimpse into his fear, and he didn't have to be afraid alone.

While anger can be a powerful fuel to propel us toward change, fear is often a paralyzing emotion. We can feel so much fear and anxiety that we are unable to move forward and remain stuck. Fear prevents us from making decisions, from saying things we need to say, from healing and change. Fear of rejection and failure keeps us from moving forward on ideas, dreams, and intimacy.

Some of us are more in touch with our fear than others; it can manifest as a low-level buzzing in our heads, a high-frequency screaming that we can't get a break from, or anything in between.

The words "Do not be afraid" are woven throughout the stories of Jesus' birth. The angels say them to Zechariah, Joseph, Mary, and the shepherds. "Joseph, son of David, do not be afraid to take Mary home as your wife" (Matthew 1:20); "Do not be afraid, Zechariah, for your prayer has been heard. Your wife Elizabeth will bear you a son" (Luke 1:13); "Do not be afraid, Mary, for you have found favor with God" (Luke 1:30); "An angel of the Lord stood before them, and the glory of the Lord shone around them, and they were terrified. But the angel said to them, 'Do not be afraid; for see — I am bringing you good news of great joy for all the people'" (Luke 2:9–10).

When I read these passages, my first response is scoffing. *Really, it's that simple? Just "don't be afraid"?* Because of misinterpretation of these Scriptures and failure to recognize the humanity in them, a lot of us have been taught that fear is a lack of trust in God—that if we just prayed harder or were more faithful and courageous, fear would magically dissipate.

I don't think that's how it works. I always remind people that *courage is doing hard things scared.* The way out of fear isn't grinding down to get rid of it but rather to acknowledge it and then consider how we can keep moving forward despite it.

This season, what are you afraid of? How is fear keeping you stuck?

Thursday
Shame

If we can share our story with someone who responds with
empathy and understanding, shame can't survive.
—Brené Brown[7]

You are defective. You are not worthy. You'll never measure up.
You'll never be enough. Who do you think you are? What's wrong
with you?

Do any of these messages sound familiar?

Shame does a number on our heads and hearts and is
often magnified during the holiday season. Perceived relational or personal failures, lack of resources, fragile faith,
or feelings of unworthiness or not being where we "should"
be in life can become more blaring. It makes us weary and
is the number-one destroyer of freedom, relationship, and
hope.

Brené Brown, one of the best voices today on shame
and vulnerability, describes the difference between guilt
and shame like this: Guilt is "I did something bad" while
shame is "I am bad."[8]

A lot of us have hidden shame—unspoken things that
are hard to say out loud, things from the past or present
we find painful to admit. They might be things under the
surface we try to keep a lid on—financial struggles, hidden
addictions, relationships falling apart, chronic pain, decon-
structing faith, mental illness. Others of us are wrestling
with openly exposed things we can't hide—divorce, way-
ward kids, losing jobs, observable struggles, lack of a faith
that is acceptable to friends and family members. While
I've spent many years working relentlessly to acknowledge the realities of shame in my life and become more
free, shame is sneaky and has tried to hook me again this
season. The loss of our son to suicide has triggered a new

layer of shame: *we must be terrible parents.* I imagine people wondering, "Who does she think she is, leading people as a pastor?"

Yeah, shame is vicious, mean, and working overtime to try to get me these days.

And probably some of you, too, who are familiar with its tentacles.

Usually our response to exposed shame is similar to the story in Genesis 1 of Adam and Eve—isolate, run, or find a weird way to cover it up.

Regardless of how we intersect with shame, it's always insidious and robs us of joy, love, and connection.

What's the way out from under shame's weight? The proper Christian answer is often "Jesus!" While I believe Jesus is the great shame destroyer, that response often perpetuates more shame and implies if we believed properly, we wouldn't feel what we're feeling. It's not that simple. One of the first steps in loosening shame's grip is acknowledging it with safe people who won't fix, minimize, or judge—to practice honesty.

As Brené Brown says, "If we can share our story with someone who responds with empathy and understanding, shame can't survive."[9]

As you practice honesty this week, where is shame rearing its head? What's rolling around in your head and heart about your value and worth?

Friday
Disorientation

*God is not distant or impassive to the pain and confusion we
are left with, but is a real and present Comforter among us.*
                                                    —Jamie Arpin-Ricci[10]

Anger, sadness, fear, shame—these are some really big feelings swirling around. No wonder we're weary! While they look different for each of us, the thread woven through them all is usually the same—they leave us feeling lost and confused. Things definitely aren't how we want them to be, we aren't sure of the way out, and it's tiring.

For many of us, when we experience a significant shift in our life or faith, when we lose all we once knew, we also lose the structures and groups we belonged to and the relationships tied to them. Those losses are difficult, but the one that gets us the most is usually what comes at the end of losing all we once knew—our identity.

Who are we when we're not who we used to be?

Who are we when we are consumed with these incredibly vulnerable feelings?

Who are we when we no longer belong to groups or systems in which we used to find safety and shelter?

Who are we when we aren't sure anymore what we even believe about God?

While Advent is a season of "waiting" for the birth of Jesus for a month, Christmas Eve is when the story is supposed to come together with Jesus' arrival. This can be confusing to a lot of us who still are left with the same realities Christmas morning—and the day after that, and the day after that. I think we've done a disservice by not acknowledging that feelings don't magically disappear when we hit a certain date on the calendar. Many biblical stories point to being lost and then found, suffering from disease and being miraculously healed, or transitioning from unbelief to belief in a matter of seconds.

I appreciate the stories and believe we're supposed to wrestle with them together, but when I'm feeling lost and confused, false platitudes to quickly shake me out of my genuinely tangled-up feelings don't help.

I know that a lot of you are tired and weary from working so hard, fighting so hard, struggling so much to keep putting one foot in front of the other with no end in sight.

We started this week with the phrase "a voice crying out in the wilderness" from Mark 1. The wilderness can be a disorienting and often terrifying place. Usually there's no road map or markers, no clear shelters, and wild animals and elements aren't only scary but are often also working against us.

It's easy to get lost in the wilderness.

Even though we might feel alone, we have a Comforter among us and a lot of fellow travelers in the wilderness.

Where do you feel lost and confused right now?

Saturday
Let's Just Be Honest . . .

*Feelings are not wrong. They're not inappropriate.
We don't need to feel guilty about feelings. . . . Feelings shouldn't be judged as either good or bad. Feelings
are emotional energy; they are not personality traits.*
                                    —Melody Beattie[11]

As we wrap up Week Two's focus on practicing honesty, I am thinking of this line in "O Holy Night": "He knows our need, To our weakness is no stranger." Anger, sadness, fear, shame, and confusion are just a few of the feelings that are often illuminated when Christmas feels blue, yet none of them are strangers to God. Each and every one of our feelings is familiar to God. I wonder how you are doing engaging with some of these primary feelings. Is it comforting? Difficult? Challenging? Healing? We all intersect with processing in our own unique ways, but as we wrestle with practicing honesty together, I hope we can feel less alone in the middle of our experience.

Recently I talked to a mom whose daughter died by suicide about six weeks after our son. The conversation was extremely raw and vulnerable, with intense pain emanating from both of our broken mama hearts—yet in the middle of deep grief there was also a solidarity and comfort in knowing we weren't alone in the feelings and could be completely and totally honest. There was no need for pretense, minimizing, or justifying. We were both able to say freely, "It's so hard, so sad, we're so mad, so hurt, so confused, so tired of not feeling like ourselves." Despite the pain, we could breathe a little easier when we said goodbye.

Knowing she exists helps me, and knowing I exist helps her.

But let's just be honest: we can't practice honesty with everyone. Not everyone is a safe person with whom to share what we're really thinking and feeling. When we're fragile, the last thing we need is someone who wants us to snap out of our feelings as quickly as possible. I know whom I can practice honesty with and whom I can't.

Often, the best place to practice first is with myself. Noticing what's really going on in my heart, living with the fullness of a wide range of emotions, and not trying to squeeze out the hard feelings are not easy tasks; my default is to fall into the trap of minimizing my emotions. In fact, I've been working on that for over two decades and still find it difficult,

What about you? How hard is it to practice honesty with yourself? With others? With God?

What helps you let your guard down and connect with what's really going on underneath the surface in a more meaningful way?

Developing a wide range of emotions is a learned skill that takes a lot of time and practice, but I hope we will all keep doing what we can to notice what's happening inside our heads and hearts and bravely express that in whatever ways help us. Maybe it's a conversation with a trusted person in our lives—a therapist or spiritual director—or expressing ourselves in our journal or through music or a visual art. There are many ways to practice honesty with our feelings of anger, sadness, fear, shame, and confusion; it's not about getting it "right" or making sure it all comes out perfectly. That's exhausting, and our weary hearts don't need more rules or expectations that squeeze hope out of our lives. We just need a way to let out some of what's inside.

When we do, we often find that in the middle of all the hard, there is good, too. We find that part of our story, God's story, the Christmas story, the human story, and the world's story is *paradox*—contradicting things existing in the same space at the same time. It's hard on a heart and soul to hold a paradox together, but it's profoundly heal-ing, too. That's what we'll dive into in Week Three. Until then, consider some of the following practices and reflec-tion questions to cultivate practicing honesty this week.

Let yourself feel what needs to be felt.

A Prayer for Practicing Honesty

God, I want to be honest.
But it's hard to be honest, too—with myself, with others,
    you.
These feelings are hard.
These feelings are real.
These feelings are scary.
Help me hold them.
Help me honor them.
Help me let you hold and honor them with me.
Help me keep practicing honesty.

To Practice

1. **Expand our repertoire of feelings.**

While we talked about some of the big feelings that a lot of us are experiencing right now, it's helpful to consider expanding our vocabulary and noticing more intentionally what we're feeling. On the next page is a chart of some of the primary feelings floating around this season (and some of which we'd like to experience more) with a few creative descriptors under each. Take some time to be quiet, noticing what's going on in your heart and soul right now. Look to see if any of these words resonate with you or what other terms might describe your feelings. Practice sharing them with a safe person, in your journal, or during a time of prayer or spiritual reflection.

2. **Smash something!**

Something about getting into our bodies and out of our heads releases pain and helps us find relief. Our Blue Christmas ornament smashing station is one idea. I've talked to people who have smashed eggs, plates, or glassware against some kind of wall or target or bought a bunch of large nails to pound into a board. The key is to do something that releases big feelings in a healthy way. Denver has a few "rage room" businesses where people can pay to smash stuff—there may be one in your hometown. There are countless ways to be creative with this concept. The essence of the practice is to let it rip in a safe space (with safety goggles on, at least), and let the feelings out that sometimes get stuck only in our minds.

3. **Consider the need underneath the feeling.**

Nonviolent Communication by Marshall Rosenberg is a book worth exploring to gain greater skill in practicing honesty and cultivating healthier relationships with ourselves, others, and God. One of the core nonviolent communication principles is that underneath every feeling is a need.[12]

SADNESS	ANGER	STRESS	SHAME	PEACE	JOY	LOVE
Depressed	Resentful	Panicky	Embarrassed	Grateful	Satisfied	Connected
Anguished	Frustrated	Apprehensive	Guilty	Strengthened	Content	Valued
Hopeless	Disgusted	Anxious	Unworthy	Determined	Excited	Respected
Heartbroken	Irritated	Lost	Powerless	Comforted	Renewed	Supported
Mournful	Furious	Defeated	Dejected	Grounded	Inspired	Comforted
Discouraged	Offended	Worried	Weak	Secure	Focused	Tender
Ignored	Rageful	Weary	Paralyzed	Strong	Hopeful	Vulnerable
Tired	Disappointed	Doubtful	Defensive	Brave	Light	Full

Despite popular belief, need is good and points to a desire for connection—with ourselves, others, and God. One thing that can really help in practicing honesty is getting in touch with some of the needs underneath our feelings. *Nonviolent Communication* offers a long list of needs to consider, but using a broad brush, some of them fall into the categories of physical needs, connection, authenticity, safety, and security. Below are a few needs to consider in each of these categories:

— *Physical needs*—food, rest, movement, sleep, shelter, touch
— *Connection and authenticity*—acceptance, affection, belonging, communication, compassion, empathy, inclusion, intimacy, love, mutuality, nurturing, respect, support, trust
— *Meaning*—clarity, competence, growth, hope, purpose, understanding
— *Autonomy*—choice, freedom, independence, space, spontaneity
— *Play*—joy, humor, creativity, curiosity
— *Peace*—beauty, ease, equality, harmony, order, security

Walk through the short guided reflection below to practice considering what needs might be underneath some of your feelings:

Take a few moments and consider how you are feeling right now. What circumstances are heavy on your heart? What relationships or situations are troubling you?

Now, consider what you might need right now. Go through the list above and circle which ones resonate.

Owning what we need doesn't mean we'll get it met, but it can open the door to asking for more specific help and clarifying what's going on underneath the surface in our hearts and souls. Use this prompt:

— *Right now, I'm feeling* _____.
— *I think I need* _____.
— *A way I might be able to get this need is* _____ [ask someone, initiate something, make time for it, etc.].

For Group Reflection

1. Practice honesty in the group together. Share this prompt: *Right now, I'm really feeling* _____ *because of* _____. Remember the guidelines for sharing: don't try to fix others' feelings, but just allow them to enter the group, honor them, and hold them together.

2. Consider fear in a more intentional way. What are we afraid of right now? How is it affecting our minds, hearts, relationships, or faith?

3. Reflect on the various feelings discussed in Week Two — anger, grief, fear, shame, and disorientation. What resonated or lingered from the daily reflections? Share with the group and notice common themes together.

WEEK THREE

Embracing Paradox

Sunday
Introduction

There is a crack, a crack in everything
That's how the light gets in.
—Leonard Cohen[1]

I mentioned previously that one of my favorite words is "practice." I recently wrote a book titled *Practicing: Changing Yourself to Change the World*, which is centered on ten important practices the world needs more of: healing, listening, loving, including, equalizing, advocating, mourning, failing, resting, and celebrating. There's another -ing concept that's an essential spiritual practice not only for when Christmas is blue but for all seasons: embracing paradox. Paradox—contradicting things existing in the same space at the same time—has taken on new meaning for us since our son died. We've felt the weight of the burden of holding a wide range of conflicting feelings in our hearts and souls. Paradox is a tricky thing to hold, so we often default to a more simplistic, dualistic, either/or thinking.

In the conservative faith system I ascribed to for a long time, either/or thinking, belief, and practice were prevalent. Things were either right or wrong, good or bad, sinful or godly, and a host of other binary choices. When I started talking to other people more bravely about my real life and struggles, I realized I wasn't alone. So many of us were wrestling with a divided life, squeezing contradictions out by swinging to one side or the other. Much of my Christian experience cemented this kind of thinking. "Gray" was considered unbiblical. "Fear" meant we weren't trusting God properly. "Anger" equated to a lack of spiritual maturity. "Doubt" indicated lack of proper faith. The result: when negative feelings arose, I'd do anything possible to work diligently and faithfully to get rid of them as quickly as possible.

This week, I couldn't help but think that one of the most important tools we can use to not only make it through the hard parts of this season—but all parts of our human experience— is the idea of *embracing paradox*. In fact, without cultivating this ability to hold together the widest possible range of experiences, peace on our journey is nearly impossible. We can't feel solid or free if we are constantly swinging from one extreme to the next, unable to hold the tension of contradictions about ourselves, others, God, and life in the same space.

Embracing paradox—both/and thinking, living, and practice—has been incredibly transforming, not only in my life but also in the lives of so many others I know.

Now I am learning to put two of my favorite words together in real life—*practicing paradox*. Trust me, it's a lot easier to say than do! In fact, it's brutally hard on a soul to live with the reality of our family's deep grief in the middle of so many positive things in our lives at the same time— vocations we love, four other young adult children launching into their careers and futures, and the birth of our new nonprofit called #communityheals, dedicated to making spaces for transformation accessible for all.

My husband and kids have all shared that we sometimes feel bad for feeling good, for smiling in pictures, for laughing when our hearts are so broken. But we are trying to learn how to practice paradox and embrace grieving and living at the same time. One feeling or reality doesn't completely discount the other; rather, they can live in the same space at the same time.

Dr. Henry Cloud, in his book *Changes That Heal*, fleshes out the idea that emotional maturity is learning how to hold good and bad in the same space.[2] When things become either "all good" or "all bad" instead of both good and bad at the same time, it's dangerous and causes us to split off parts of ourselves in a destructive way. Life is never all good or all bad, all dark or all light.

Even in the darkest of dark days after losing our son, there was and is light—people's tenderness toward us, whispers of love, hugs from our kids, the unconditional love of our dog, the sunrise every morning. These glimmers—mixed in with the worst of the worst—have sustained us.

However, looking for light doesn't mean we minimize, dismiss, or rationalize the dark. We don't try to squeeze it out, only focus on the good, or toss in a few Scriptures to make it all better. No, the dark and light need to exist together—the hard and the good, the beauty and the mess, peace and chaos, hope and despair, love and hate coexisting in our own lives, in the people around us, and in the wider world.

Embracing paradox has a ripple effect—but like all things, it always starts with ourselves. Father Richard Rohr says, "If you can hold and forgive the contradictions within yourself, you can normally do it everywhere else, too."[3]

Yes, embracing paradox can make us weary. Really, I just want the grief to be finally *done* so that I can be back to all of the good that existed before that tragic day, but I know that's only a falsity that feels comforting. Even before Jared died, we were holding all kinds of contradictions together in our lives and souls. It's part of every human experience, and now it's just massively amplified. I am finding that holding this much pain creates a mysterious and holy space. Mirabai Starr, an interspiritual professor and author, reminds us, "The path of the mystic reconciles contradictory propositions (such as harrowing sorrow and radical amazement) and blesses us with an expanded capacity to sit with ambiguity, to treasure vulnerability, to celebrate paradox as the highest truth."[4]

She goes on to say, "We are conditioned to see death and painful longing as problems to be solved rather than as sacred landscapes to be revered. We are encouraged to medicate our grief, to treat loss as a malfunction that needs troubleshooting, to satisfy our longing as swiftly as possible."[5]

A lot of our Christian Western culture teaches us either/or thinking and that all our dissonance is something to be resolved as quickly as possible—yet almost all of the ways of Jesus embody both/and rather than either/or.

Jesus' birth doesn't make sense in some ways and brings it all together in another. It's ugly and smelly and also beautiful and hopeful. Three decades later, Jesus—the one who was supposed to save the day with kingly strength and might—dies on a cross, leaving so many even more confused. The essence of the Jesus story is that we rise by descending. It's a mystery, yet it's simple. It's easy to talk about and hard to live out. I'm sure you can think of a lot of other contrary words to describe it.

As we travel this road toward Christmas, my hope for myself, my family, and those who are struggling with this season is to try and embrace the paradoxes of our own lives, people we're connected to, and the wider world.

Here's why. Embracing paradox can help us to

— Learn to accept all parts of ourselves instead of rejecting our weaknesses and being mad at God and ourselves for not "fixing ourselves" quickly enough.
— Develop keener eyes to see together the beauty and the ugliness (and all the other kinds of wild

contradictions that exist) in other people (and institutions, too) instead of only focusing on one or the other.
— Increase the capacity for grace for ourselves and others. There's no downside to cultivating more grace in this harsh world.
— Stop setting ourselves up in relationships where we're the all-good or the all-bad person.
— Develop a resiliency that is impossible when we demand things to be either/or. We can see joy in suffering, peace in tribulations, and wholeness and healing in brokenness.
— Widen our ability to intersect with people very different from us. This is essential for a life of downward mobility and incarnational living.

I'm guessing this idea of paradox isn't new to many of you; you have been holding contradictory things together in your story for a long time. Regardless, no matter how much we *know* we need to hold paradox, it's much simpler to talk about it in an intellectual sense than to truly embrace it in the crevices of our hearts and our experiences.

The lectionary passage for this third week of Advent includes Mary's Magnificat, sprinkled with paradox. She sings,

"He has brought down the powerful from their thrones,
    and lifted up the lowly;
he has filled the hungry with good things,
    and sent the rich away empty." (Luke 1:52–53)

In this third week together, we'll walk through embracing paradox during this season and remember there's light in the darkness, beautiful in the ugly, peace in chaos, and hope in despair.

What contradictory feelings or qualities do you notice within yourself?

Monday
Light and Dark

"The world is indeed full of peril, and in it there are many dark places; but still there is much that is fair, and though in all lands love is now mingled with grief, it grows perhaps the greater."
—J. R. R. Tolkien[6]

At The Refuge we sometimes do community labyrinth walks at different locations in North Denver. These contemplative experiences of walking a winding path quietly are always healing. There's something about the twists, the turns, the quiet, and the space to hear from God in interesting ways that always seems to come at the right time. One morning I was walking a local labyrinth carrying big burdens of a broken relationship in my life. Everything felt dark and draining, and my soul was heavy, my mind scattered. As I was making a few of the first turns I heard these words in the quiet corner of my heart: "Kathy, look toward the light."

Look toward the light.

Instead of pushing this thought down, I listened, and each time I made a turn on the labyrinth, I intentionally stopped and turned my whole body and head up toward the sun.

Look toward the light.

Labyrinths are full of turns, so I stopped a lot that morning. Even when I felt like just keeping my head down and getting to the center as fast as I could, I made myself stop, turn my head up, and look to the light.

Everything didn't change. My circumstances didn't magically disappear. My pain and struggle certainly were not suddenly gone. But I noticed something significant as I exited: my head was higher, my shoulders were less slumped, and I felt a little lighter.

Light is powerful. Light is healing. Light is hope.

We can look toward it, even in the darkest of seasons. In the northern hemisphere, where Christmas originated, the nights in December are the longest of the year; many of us feel the shift that happens on the Winter Solstice when each next day we gain a little more light than on the previous one. Looking toward the light in the dark season of the holidays or in our life circumstances can be different for all of us. Maybe it's gratitude; maybe it's something we see or read that warms our heart; maybe it's a small kindness, a tender word, an animal's unconditional love, a song that stirs us.

Look toward the light.

I'm not saying that if we just "look to the light," everything will be okay. There's no question that everything in my life right now is So. Not. Okay. The darkness, pain, struggle, reality, and feelings can still exist—and I can notice the light.

My hope is that in the middle of our weary world we'd stop, beckon our heads to look up, and turn our hearts, minds, and bodies toward the light. To remember the things that *are* instead of only the things that *aren't*, that "The world is indeed full of peril, and in it there are many dark places; but still there is much that is fair."[7]

What are some slivers of light you are seeing in the midst of the darkness right now?

Tuesday
Beautiful and Ugly

For the sake of your heart and all
You should own your name
And stand up tall and get real
See the beauty in ugly.

—Jason Mraz[8]

On the most surface of levels, giving birth is not the prettiest picture—blood, pain, sweat, moaning. It's messy and grueling. Having given birth to five children with no pain medication, I can also say without a doubt that it hurts—a lot! But at the same time—in the middle of the hard, ugly, and painful—it's one of the most beautiful, tender, amazing gifts on earth.

I often think of Mary giving birth to Jesus, surrounded by animals, smells, and sounds that weren't sterile or shiny. We have so few concrete details of her experience, but we do know that it was human, messy, bloody, dirty, sweet, and miraculous at the same time.

Like our lives.

Embracing the paradox that beautiful can exist in the middle of life's ugliness can be extremely healing. We see it in far more places than a birthing room: when we are walking on concrete sidewalks and notice tiny flowers peeking through, when we experience a tenderness or kind word in a crowded line of people, when we hear a story of good news in a world screaming with bad.

Beautiful in the ugly.

It's hard to see sometimes, and like the darkness, the ugliness often blinds us to any of the good. When our own lives feel dim, especially in contrast to the shininess of the holiday festivities, it's tempting to tune it all out and let everything become an ugly blur.

A few weeks ago, I was at the house of a friend who is struggling with significant health issues. He is a disabled war veteran with severe PTSD, and his quality of life at this stage of his story is very low. Sitting in his tiny subsidized apartment with ashtrays full of cigarette butts and mess all around, he asked me if I wanted to hear a poem he wrote. I have known him for sixteen years, and he has never shared anything like this, so I was a little stunned. He expressed that he had suddenly felt like writing and bought himself one of those little black and white composition books for a dollar. As I listened to his beautiful words, raw and real, expressing his wounds and hope tangled up together, it was truly holy. With tears streaming down my face as I heard his ragged, rough voice speak such glory, I was reminded there's so much beautiful in the ugly, so much holy in the hard, so much tenderness in the brutal.

Sometimes we have to strain to see it. Sometimes it will appear out of nowhere. It can't be forced, but we can be open. It helps weary hearts keep going.

Where are you seeing beauty in the ugly?

Wednesday
Peace and Chaos

For a child has been born for us,
a son given to us;
authority rests upon his shoulders;
and he is named
Wonderful Counselor, Mighty God,
Everlasting Father, Prince of Peace.

—Isaiah 9:6

The political climate in the United States for the past number of years has been tumultuous, chaotic, unpredictable, and downright exhausting. The constantly changing news cycles and the deep divisions within groups, families, and friends have created a lot of fear, anxiety, and despair in so many people. During this book's production, we are a few months into the coronavirus pandemic and fears for our future are rising. We are wondering, *Will the churn ever end? Is this how life is going to be now? How can we find rest in the middle of the unrelenting storm? Is peace even possible?*

I once bought a greeting card that I kept for myself that says, "Peace doesn't mean the absence of noise, trouble or hard work. It means to be in the midst of those things and still have calm in your heart."

Can we truly find peace in the middle of the chaos?

Like all things related to human struggles, peace does not drop out of the sky and magically appear. Nor do I think that if we pray, meditate, exercise, talk to our therapist, read our Bible, or believe certain things enough that perfect peace is somehow guaranteed.

Yet I also truly believe that peace is possible in the middle of chaos, because I can feel it myself.

In the middle of the deepest, most brutal storms of our lives, we also feel a strange sense of somehow being anchored to peace, tethered to the story of human beings' suffering and survival throughout the ages.

For me, one of the most compelling images of peace in chaos is a tree in a winter storm—harsh and cold winds whipping through, yet still rooted; battered, bruised, its branches starkly stripped of leaves but somehow still standing, planted into the earth, gathering an unexplainable strength from the Source. Surviving, enduring, living despite it all.

Peace doesn't mean our circumstances will change.

Peace doesn't mean our hearts are completely still and settled.

Peace doesn't mean we are filled with some brand of false serenity.

Peace doesn't mean we don't still weep or wail or feel afraid.

Peace means that in the middle of the storm we can be strengthened by God, by something bigger than us, by the comfort and presence of the Holy Spirit, the Prince of Peace—and that we can be rooted, grounded, and tethered in the midst of chaos.

How are you finding peace in the middle of the chaos?

Thursday
Hope and Despair

But God will never forget the needy;
the hope of the afflicted will never perish.
—Psalm 9:18 (NIV)

I often tell people, "Hope is dangerous." Hope is an easy word to toss around: "hold on to hope," "don't lose hope," "there's always hope." For many, it gets lost in the cacophony of trite spiritual phrases they're tired of hearing.

I also cringe when I hear "hope" misused but readily admit it's still one of my favorite words. My friends have teased me about it for years, but they also know that I have never had a happy-clappy hope that "everything happens for a reason" or "everything works out in the end" or "our hope is in heaven." This hope I hold is the deepest kind, convincing me that in the middle of the darkest night, the most extreme despair, the worst of the worst, there's also fuel that keeps us going—that life is worth living; that humans can hold profound suffering and sustaining resilience at the same time; that, in the words of the psalmist, "the hope of the poor [shall not] perish forever."

I love what Anne Lamott says: "Hope is not about proving anything. It's about choosing to believe this one thing, that love is bigger than any grim, bleak shit anyone can throw at us."[9]

Hope is vulnerable, yet it can exist in the middle of despair because hope doesn't mean that everything turns out the way we want, that we're exempt from pain, that we won't suffer, that we won't ache in every part of our bones for the rest of our lives, that mental illness will be healed, that chronic pain will disappear, that we'll get that job we really want, that our family will stop being so dysfunctional, that our candidate will win, or that everything will smooth out over time.

At The Refuge, I like to encourage us all to remember that hope is a precious commodity and we need to notice, call out, draw out, celebrate, cling to, and do anything we possibly can to remember it.

To celebrate hope where we see it, no matter how big or small. To not be afraid of it.

Here are some of the places I'm seeing hope right now in the middle of so much churn, despair, struggle, loss, confusion, and division:

In people, surviving hard things, as I am.

In protests, with advocates and activists fighting for justice and change.

In my kids, who despite suffering the loss of their brother, are deeply dedicated to keep living and dreaming and working toward social change even though they are hurting.

In Jared's friends, who are committed to doing their own healing and grieving, and intend to continue his legacy, carrying on his call that "we can't change the world but we can change someone's world."

In my Refuge friends, who are struggling in so many ways yet care for one another, serve in our community, and keep moving forward even when they're tired.

In the truth that *hope can live alongside despair.*

Where are you seeing hope right now?

Friday
Love and Hate

We must be intentional about exploring the real issues of our lives: faith and fear, hope and despair, love and hate, among others.
—Parker Palmer[10]

My friend Marty is one of the kindest and most loving humans I know. She cares deeply for people and is always willing to listen, love, support, encourage, and help. When I think of Marty, I think of the word *love*. Yet as a left-leaning progressive voter, she has struggled deeply with Donald Trump being elected president of the United States in 2016 and the reality of so many policies being implemented that violate her core values.

She's owned her feelings, saying, "I don't want to hate, but that's what this feels like."

I know she's not the only one.

No matter which side you are on politically or theologically, sometimes there are just things that we truly hate, even though we know we're *not supposed to*. When my kids were younger, I wouldn't let them use the word *hate*. I didn't want to perpetuate it, and after all these years, I still don't like it.

Yet I want to acknowledge that it's a real feeling for a lot of us for many different reasons.

Maybe it's an ex-spouse or significant other or family member or coworker or political figure. Or maybe it's a reality in your life that you would give anything to be rid of. Maybe it's ourselves—one of the easiest things in the world to hate. I was good at that one for a long time.

I don't want to promote hate, but I want to acknowledge that if we do indeed feel it, it doesn't mean we can't also feel love, too. Sometimes underneath hate are all kinds of other feelings: fear, confusion, concern, care, violation, anger, injustice.

Owning that these big feelings can exist in the same space as love is part of spiritual and emotional maturity. It can help us be less hard on ourselves, on others, and on God, too. God's love is for everyone. Yes, there are Scriptures that point to things that "God hates," but that's not the full story. I believe that the full story—the gospel in a nutshell—is that nothing, absolutely nothing, can separate us from God's love. Romans 8:38 reminds us, "I am convinced that neither death nor life, nor rulers, nor things present, nor things to come, nor powers, nor height, nor depth, nor anything else in all creation will be able to separate us from the love of God in Christ Jesus our Lord."

No matter how much we struggle with harsh and hard feelings toward people, groups, institutions, and even ourselves—love is bigger than it all and can hold us even when we can't.

Be honest about what you feel like you hate right now. What do you love at the same time?

Saturday
Let's Just Be Honest . . .

When I get honest, I admit I am a bundle of paradoxes.
I believe and I doubt, I hope and get discouraged, I love and
I hate, I feel bad about feeling good, I feel guilty about not
feeling guilty. I am trusting and suspicious. I am honest and
I still play games. Aristotle said I am a rational animal;
I say I am an angel with an incredible capacity for beer.
— Brennan Manning[11]

Let's just be honest—it's easier to talk about paradox than actually embrace it. But part of our spiritual and personal transformation is to open ourselves up to being able to hold these radically contradictory things in tension in our own hearts, lives, and souls, and the experiences of others and the wider world, too. We can be simultaneously weak and strong; in the middle of darkness, there can still be light; there's beautiful in the ugly, peace amid the chaos. Hope can exist alongside our deepest despair, and we can simultaneously feel love and hate.

Embracing paradox isn't just a theory; it's a spiritual practice not only present in the Christian faith or the Christmas story but expressed in every world religion in different ways. It's part of the human experience, and the current renewed emphasis that's happening now on mindfulness, contemplative prayer, and breaking out of dualistic thinking is centered on helping us as humans hold more naturally this important spiritual truth.

When Christmas is blue, when our hearts are weary, when the pain of the world can feel so consuming, hopeless, and brutal, embracing paradox can help sustain us.

We can remember that God is paradoxical, we are paradoxical, life is paradoxical—all kinds of contradictory things can exist in the same place at the same time, none discounting the other, none needing to squeeze out the other, none needing to be prayed out. Instead, our prayers can be focused on gaining strength, courage, wisdom, and hope to hold it all.

As we wrap up Week Three, I hope we can make friends with paradox, welcome the fullness of all our experiences, and embrace our own and others' contradictions. It makes me think of the wise words of the Sufi poet Rumi in his poem "The Guest House" about the wide range of human experiences that visit us each day—"Welcome and entertain them all!"[12]

A Prayer for Embracing Paradox

God, all these contradictory feelings swirling around are
    rough on our souls.
Help us hold them all.
Help us remember in the middle of grief, we can still live.
In the middle of despair, we can still hope.
In the middle of chaos, peace is still possible.
In the middle of division, love still lives.
Give us courage to own our paradoxical story.
Help us remember yours.

To Practice

1. Embrace paradox in your life right now by considering your story and sharing it with someone else.

Using the prompt below if you need a little help, consider the contradictory feelings or realities you are living out right now. Choose one word from the left column and one word from the right, or use any of your own.

Right now, my story is _____ *and* _____.

Our Stories

abundant	ambivalent
alive	angry
awake	apprehensive
beautiful	bound
compassionate	broken
connected	bumpy
creative	challenging
curious	closed
delighted	confusing
easy	dark
empowered	dead
encouraging	depressing
free	empty
fulfilled	exhausting
full	fierce
genuine	frustrating
glorious	hard
grateful	heavy
light	insecure
loud	irritating
noble	lonely
open	messy
pretty	sorry

proud	scattered
quiet	shattered
redeemed	tired
resilient	turbulent
restored	ugly
revived	unnerved
safe	unsettled
satisfied	vulnerable
secure	visceral
smooth	wandering
strong	weak
tenacious	weary
whole	wondering

Tell a trusted person in your life what you're learning about embracing paradox, what's hard, what's good, and how they can support you in holding these radically different feelings in tension.

2. Embrace paradox in other places, too.

Consider something outside of your story that you are wrestling with right now—political division, family struggles, a broken relationship. Can you name some of the contradictory feelings about them? _____ [The situation, person, institution, group] *is both* _____ *and* _____. Consider how your feelings might shift by recognizing the both/and instead of the either/or.

3. Actively seek healing in art, music, or nature.

Find a piece of art or music or a symbol in nature that represents paradox in your life right now or make one of your own. What does it symbolize? What stirs your soul? What helps embody this idea?

For Group Reflection

1. Share some of your both/ands with the group. Consider these prompts:

Right now, my story is _____ and _____.
I'm feeling _____ and _____.
I'm grieving _____ and also celebrating _____.

2. With which of the reflections in Week Three did you most identify? Share why and what was stirred up in you.

3. Take some time together and write down all of the current feelings, struggles, celebrations, and messy and beautiful things happening in the group right now. Say them out loud and put them all on a big piece of paper or in one place so that the entire group can see how they can exist in the same space at the same time. If you'd like, offer thanks together or pray for strength to hold these together in the week ahead.

WEEK FOUR

Borrowing Hope

Sunday
Introduction

"We need more hope. We need more mercy. We need more justice."
—Bryan Stevenson[1]

Years ago, my friend Tami, who is an amazingly resilient mom of five who continues to heal from a lifetime of trauma and abuse and is finding her way, shared with me, "Kathy, I just need to borrow some hope from you guys right now. I've lost mine." Sometimes we need to borrow hope from each other. In that moment, she had to borrow some from us—her friends in community—and at other times I've borrowed some from her.

In the middle of real life, real struggles, real loss, real crises of faith, and real humanity, it's easy to become weary, exhausted, and hopeless. Sometimes one of the only things that can sustain us comes from other people or God or an inspiration that helps us take the next breath or the next step, or make it through the next day.

This final week of Advent we'll consider ways to borrow hope. Hope means different things for people, but for a lot of us it's some kind of expectation—a possibility that maybe things could be different, that there's more to life than what we see, that there's something better ahead. Many of us, for all kinds of reasons, are afraid to hope.

We have seen many of our dreams dashed, our jobs lost, our relationships crumble, our health deteriorate, addictions ravage, and God not delivering the goods the way we had hoped. Because of past experiences, we then hunker down in our hearts and do whatever we can to protect them against believing that good is actually possible. We settle for loneliness, disconnectedness, and going through the motions.

Often the thought of something more hurts too much. The thought of making ourselves vulnerable and getting hurt again is too risky. The what-ifs mount, hope gets held at bay, and we miss out on the thing that Jesus kept pointing to over and over again in the Gospels—life now, love now, hope now—despite our circumstances. I am constantly reminded that pretty much everything Jesus calls people to is quite dangerous. Why would hope be different?

Hope requires risk and sacrifice. Working against our reflexes to run, hide, self-protect, and self-medicate, hope requires believing in what is unseen. It means we will hurt. It means we will be afraid. It will mean taking steps on an unfamiliar path. Hope will require letting God's spirit move in ways that feel mysterious, scary, and often unfamiliar. So how do we get over our fear of hope's dangerousness? How do we borrow hope?

Maybe, in whatever our feeble ways, we could try the following:

Admit what we're really afraid of. Is it being afraid to fail? Or our hearts hurting? Being certain we'll just end up mad at God again? What freaks us out about hope?

Seek courage in the small steps. We sometimes have relentlessly high expectations of ourselves, that we're supposed to somehow "take the hill" or "win the race" or "have it mastered" tomorrow. This kind of all-or-none thinking usually leads us to failure, shame, and anger toward ourselves for our lack of faith and courage. Small steps keep hope alive, especially when we celebrate them in community.

Expect hope to hurt. Self-protection keeps us sealed off; hope makes us more vulnerable.

Recognize that hope in circumstances is not reliable. We often rest our hope in outcomes, tangibles, ideals of how we think they should turn out instead of in the mystery of God and things we will never truly know.

Strain to see God, feel God, hear God wherever we can. We get so blinded by our pain, fear, busyness, and self-preservation that it becomes difficult to experience God's spirit moving, revealing, challenging, strengthening, encouraging, and healing. Especially when hope is waning and our anger or ambivalence is getting the best of us, we will need to strain to see God in small, simple ways that might normally be missed. Maybe it's in the eyes of a friend, a word of encouragement, a song, a view of the mountains, a crisis, Scripture, a poem, or absolutely anything that stirs our hearts toward love, hope, and joy.

There's no question that hope is dangerous. Hope can't be rushed, forced, or cajoled into us. I'm also reminded that the lectionary passage for this last week of Advent includes Luke 1:37: "Nothing will be impossible with God." Please know I'm not trying to say, "If you just do this, hope will come." But what I believe in every part of my soul—from my own current experience and walking with so many others through pain, suffering, wrestling, doubt, confusion, and healing—is that sometimes I need to borrow some hope to make it through the day. My guess is that some of you do, too.

Who or what are you borrowing hope from right now?

Monday
Love in Action

The life of the soul is not knowledge, it is love. . . ."
—Thomas Merton[2]

While I'm not a big fan of Christmas carols, I have never minded singing them, and there's something special about people throughout generations singing the same songs at the same time of year. For me, they don't have the same trigger as certain worship songs that often imply that if we just trust God and worship God enough, everything will be okay. At the same time, "Joy to the World" doesn't really feel appropriate when your soul is gutted by the loss of a child.

However, the song that inspired the title of this book is one that truly stirs my soul ever year, and this past Christmas Eve was no different. My favorite lines in "O Holy Night" are these:

> Truly He taught us to love one another;
> His law is Love and His gospel is Peace;
> Chains shall he break, for the slave is our brother,
> And in his name all oppression shall cease.[3]

As much as my faith has shifted and some of our dreams have been shattered, I still hold on to these deeper truths: *He taught us to love one another. His law is love. His gospel is peace.*

Each and every day I see the power of love manifested in healing community. People of all shapes, sizes, and experiences sharing their hearts with each other, supporting each other in the darkest nights and celebrating the smallest victories. In the middle of the world's endless churn, there are still countless people across ages, beliefs, socioeconomics, political persuasions, and life experiences truly dedicated to loving people despite the costs. There are so many community organizers, activists, caregivers, nonprofit leaders, first responders, and case workers laboring tirelessly to serve people, change unjust laws, and practice the law of love.

It's easy to forget when we see a seemingly never-ending cycle of hate, injustice, oppression, and pain, but it's something from which we can borrow hope. Despite unjust systems continuing to thrive, many people continue to determinedly labor on behalf of love; who care deeply for the poor; who advocate for those on the underside of power; who risk their egos, positions, and paychecks to embody a better way; who do whatever they can to break someone's chains.

My son was one of those people; since his death, we are still receiving poignant cards and letters from both kids and grown-ups telling us how Jared loved them in beautiful and tangible ways that made a significant impact in their lives.

Love in action gives me hope.

Where are you seeing love in action?

Tuesday
Still, We Rise

*You may trod me in the very dirt
But still, like dust, I'll rise.*

— Maya Angelou[4]

If you're like me, some days feel incredibly discouraging. Listening to the news makes us feel like the world is on a trajectory of destruction. Our social media feeds magnify it even more. The angst, division, wars, suffering, and violence are often too much to bear. We want to tune it out, put our fingers in our ears, and do whatever we can to still believe there's good in the world despite the hard.

I am not certain of much, but there *is* good in the world despite the hard.

Since Jared's death, I've been a bit obsessed with considering all the people who have endured brutal hardships not only in history but in current events, too. The ravages of slavery, wars, violence, pandemics, and natural disasters are woven throughout the ages, yet one thing continues to remain: people's tenacity to keep going, to make it out of their countries to provide a better life for their children, rebuilding amid the rubble and ruins of losing everything, no matter how small the everything was.

Humans are incredible like that.

We endure.

We survive.

We find ways to keep going.

We hope against all odds.

Brené Brown warns us against what she calls "comparative suffering,"[5] where we minimize our suffering because it's not as hard or big or real or worthy as others' suffering. I agree with her completely; it's crucial to not look at others and minimize our pain. As a white, educated, privileged, married, straight woman, it's easy to engage in comparative suffering. I am connected to many vulnerable people with no resources, and I have every opportunity for healing at my fingertips, yet it's comforting to know humanity's legacy is that generations upon generations have survived the worst possible disasters and keep rising out of the ash heap of pain and loss.

My dear friend Stacy is an abuse survivor, a grief therapist for kids, and also The Refuge's kids' pastor. An only child, her single mom was her sole living family member and she died of breast cancer when Stacy was twenty-two. I know so many people like Stacy, adult orphans, who don't have any biological family as a safety net; yet, despite all the obstacles and insecurities, they keep going. Stacy keeps rising, crawling her way toward healing, and cultivating her "chosen family," of which I am honored to be part. The holidays are some of her bluest times, a reminder of the loneliness and loss. But over the years she's found a way to respect her painful legacy, build in spaces to grieve this month, and also rise out of bed and into the arms of people who love her.

Who or what is helping you still rise, giving you hope?

Wednesday
Just Breathe

Breathing in. Breathing out. Be here now.
—Heatherlyn, "Be Here Now"[6]

I always remember the wise words of my yoga teacher a few years ago: "When all else fails, go back to these two simple things—breathe and drink water." Breathe and drink water. Breathing is one of the most crucial elements of being human, yet it's also one we can easily forget. Under stress, anxiety, pain, and strife, breathing is often one of the first things to go. Our breath becomes shallow, the ground underneath us becomes shaky, and we lose some of the energy we desperately need to keep going. Our breath is our built-in, on-demand nervous system regulator.

Breathing helps us get in touch with our body, the earth, our souls, our present.

Intertwined with mindfulness, breathing brings us into the here and now—not the past, which can be filled with all of the *would-haves*, *could-haves*, and *should-haves*, or the future, which is packed with *what-ifs* and a host of other things that are out of our control.

Part of borrowing hope can be the simple practice of staying in the present, just as we are. My friend Heatherlyn is a beautiful singer-songwriter, and her song "Be Here Now" is one of my favorites. Consider these lyrics:

> Welcome yourself, your whole self here—
> Being breathed. Being healed.
> Giving time no mind for a little while
> No certain way you need to be.[7]

"No certain way you need to be."

Sometimes we get so caught up in what we think we should or shouldn't be doing, how we should or shouldn't be, how we should or shouldn't feel, that we lose our ground, our breath, our center.

Breathing in and breathing out are sometimes all we can do, and that's enough.

In the first few weeks after Jared died, I received a message from a kindred writing friend that has sweetly sustained me over these months. She wrote, "Remember, Kathy, every breath you take in the face of this brutal loss is a victory. Every breath a victory." It has helped me through each of the days where, really, the only thing I could do was keep taking a next breath and nothing else. There was and is no certain way I needed to be, need to be. I can only do what I can, when I can, how I can.

Loss and pain look different for each of us, but I also know that in the face of every real human struggle — including addictions, broken relationships, angst and worry, exhaustion, disconnectedness, and grief—the same principle exists. Every breath we keep taking is a victory.

Breathe in. Breathe out. Be here now.

Thursday
A Time for Everything

For everything there is a season, and a time
for every matter under heaven:
a time to be born, and a time to die;
a time to plant, and a time to pluck up what is planted;
a time to kill, and a time to heal;
a time to break down, and a time to build up;
a time to weep, and a time to laugh;
a time to mourn, and a time to dance;
a time to throw away stones, and a time to gather stones together;
a time to embrace, and a time to refrain from embracing;
a time to seek, and a time to lose;
a time to keep, and a time to throw away;
a time to tear, and a time to sew;
a time to keep silence, and a time to speak;
a time to love, and a time to hate;
a time for war, and a time for peace.
— Ecclesiastes 3:1–10

I am an extremely loyal person. I will stick with friends through thick and thin, sometimes to my detriment. Years ago, a friend in whom I had invested a lot of emotional energy over many years disconnected from me and my family. It was distressing on a lot of complicated levels, but there was little I could do about it except to honor my feelings and practice the art of letting go—one of the hardest things for me to do. As a codependent, adult child of an alcoholic, and Enneagram Type 2, I will do just about anything to stay in relationship with people.

This Ecclesiastes 3 passage still remains as a soul-healer because it reminds me that there are seasons for everything. Some things aren't forever. Some things are beyond our control. Sometimes, no matter how hard we try and how much blood, sweat, and tears we put into a relationship, project, ministry, or dream, it just doesn't turn out the way we had hoped.

One way we can borrow hope is to remember there's a time and season for everything.

When we moved from San Diego to Colorado over two decades ago, I remember how hard it was to enter into a place with four seasons. I was used to one—warm and sunny. Getting used to four was a stretch, but as each year goes by, I have come to embrace the beauty and message of seasons—these unique times and rhythms of life that deserve to be properly honored and are all part of the bigger story.

This doesn't mean that particular times don't hurt more than others.

That it isn't brutal work to let go of hopes, dreams, relationships.

That we won't struggle with the grief associated with saying good-bye to one season and entering another.

It just means that we can learn to accept that there's a time for everything.

What is this time for you? A time to _____ *and a time to* _____.

Friday
Meeting Calamity with Serenity

God, grant me the serenity
To accept the things I cannot change
Courage to change the things I can
And wisdom to know the difference.

—from Alcoholics Anonymous,
attributed to Reinhold Niebuhr

Twelve-step recovery meetings are one of the best places on the planet to borrow hope. Hearing others' stories; sitting in a circle with fellow strugglers who share their experience, strength, and hope; and gathering tangible tools for change can offer the sustenance we sometimes need to keep going. I have been attending twelve-step meetings for codependence for over sixteen years now, and each and every time I am reminded of the courage and tenacity of human beings and the spiritual transformation that happens through this simple gathering.

At the beginning of each of our Wednesday House of Refuge gatherings at our house, we read a short reminder of why we gather and what to expect. Although the group is centered on spiritual formation and not specifically around recovery, we adapted one line from the preamble to many Alcoholics Anonymous (AA) meetings, and it's one of my favorite lines. "We are learning to match calamity with serenity."

There's a lot of calamity in the world—not only in our personal lives but in the lives of friends and family members and the communities in which we live and move. Racism, sexism, and discrimination against LGBTQ+ folks seem to prevail. Violence and climate change continue to increase at a rapid rate. Radically conflicting narratives about world events illuminate our divisions. It's rattling.

Yet all over the world, in eclectic pockets of healing, people are getting sober, breaking destructive patterns, healing deep wounds, and learning to meet calamity with serenity.

It reminds me of Jesus' words in John 14:27 from the last night with his disciples before he was betrayed and arrested: "Peace I leave with you; my peace I give to you. I do not give to you as the world gives. Do not let your hearts be troubled, and do not let them be afraid."

Serenity doesn't mean inaction. It doesn't mean apathy. It doesn't mean disconnecting from pain. It doesn't mean we stay in a circle and only focus on ourselves. It doesn't mean we avoid working hard to change unhealthy relationship patterns in our lives. It means that in the middle of the hard, we can work toward meeting calamity with serenity. We can begin to accept the things we cannot change, gain courage to change the things we can, and ask God for wisdom to know the difference. When it comes to issues of injustice, meeting calamity with serenity could also look like these words in a meme that often floats around social media that's an adaptation of the Serenity Prayer: "I am no longer accepting the things I cannot change. I am changing the things I cannot accept."

What could meeting calamity with serenity look like for you right now?

Saturday
Let's Just Be Honest . . .

Long lay the world in sin and error pining,
'Till he appeared and the soul felt its worth.
A thrill of hope the weary world rejoices,
For yonder breaks a new and glorious morn.
— Adolphe Adam, "O Holy Night"[8]

As we wrap up this last week of our short journey together, I am struck by the reality of how all of us reading with each other this season are in such radically different places. Each of our stories is stunningly unique. The range of emotions we're feeling is wide. The realities we're living out are diverse. Plus, the ways we are all coping with them are vastly different. But we can borrow some hope through loving one another and remembering we are part of a long story of human beings enduring hardship and heartbreak, remaining in the present when every part of us wants to focus on the past or stress about the future, honoring the seasons of life, learning to meet calamity with serenity, feeling our soul's worth.

Hope isn't something that can be mastered. We can't will ourselves to hope, but we can be open to it. I also believe one of the best ways to borrow hope during this blue season is to tenderly open ourselves to wonder.

Some other words for wonder include *awe, astonishment, curiosity, doubt, fascination, fear, reverence, shock, uncertainty, marveling.* When I think of the Christmas story, I see slivers of wonder in almost every character involved—Joseph, Mary, the shepherds, the magi, even King Herod.

Over the years as my faith shifted, I lost a lot of wonder. My heart is not as soft toward God, my faith glasses are foggy, and even though I abhor certainty, in some ways I have adopted a different kind of certainty. *I've become certain that I won't ever feel what I felt about church again, certain that I can't quite trust inspiration, certain that I don't believe certain things I used to be certain about.* Some days I feel certain I'll never be able to dream again, that this heart-shattering grief will never lessen, that my thoughts will always be this tangled.

The opposite of certainty is wonder.

This season, despite my aching heart and a broken world, I want to consider the word *wonder* more. It painfully but beautifully reminds me of Jared—his curiosity and openness to take in all things, ask questions, and to be present—and helps my weary heart become a little softer toward the future. One of the phrases he was known for throughout his circle of friends was, "Be interested, not interesting."

Be interested, not interesting.

Wonder. Being open. Asking questions. Becoming curious. Letting ourselves be drawn in. Not having it all have to make sense. These things are all embodied in the Christmas story; it's a story of wonder, openness, humility—of *awe, curiosity, doubt, fascination, fear, reverence, shock, uncertainty, marveling.*

In conversations with people who are wounded by the church and wonder if they've lost it all forever, I sometimes share, "Whatever you do, don't let them take your faith." What I mean is, don't let the systems of church, the people who claim to represent God, or the dysfunction of religion ruin you. I think an important variation for all of us who feel stuck in numerous ways this season might be, "Whatever we do, don't lose our sense of wonder."

Wonder can help with our weary souls.

Wonder can help in our weary world.

This Christmas and in the year ahead, I want to be as open as I can to wonder. I want to live with my *I don't knows*, ask better questions, let myself be awed by the mystery of God, be curious, be shocked, be astonished, marvel, let go of certainty-about-not-being-certain, be open, taste and experience and consider Jesus in new ways that cause my life to come more alive as we find a way to keep grieving and living at the same time.

I don't know what wonder might look like for you, but during these longest nights when we are bleeding, broken, hurting, weary, scared, and lost, I hope some wonder can make its way toward us and offer some hope.

Mary Oliver is one of my favorite poets, and in her poem "Sometimes" this short phrase hangs by itself: "melancholy leaves me breathless."[9]

Let's just be honest: melancholy does often leave us breathless.

Yet we're not left there. Later in the poem she offers these two modest but mighty lines to borrow hope from.

Be astonished.
Tell about it.[10]

A Prayer for Borrowing Hope

God, I need to borrow some hope—
from you, from others.
Help me remember that love still exists,
that people endure,
that you have been at work in the world
since the beginning of time.
May we keep rising out of the ashes,
honoring the changing seasons of our lives.
May you infuse us with courage
to keep meeting calamity with serenity.
May we be open to wonder and awe
as we keep finding our way.

To Practice

1. Practice *Lectio Divina* using these suggested Scriptures or the words to "O Holy Night."

Read your selection slowly three times, noticing what words or phrases resonate and what feelings they stir up in you. Are there any parts that bring a little hope or light?

Scripture suggestions: Psalm 23; Psalm 40; Psalm 139; Isaiah 61:1–11; Matthew 5:3–10; 1 Corinthians 13:1–13.

"O Holy Night"
O holy night, the stars are brightly shining,
It is the night of the dear Saviour's birth;
Long lay the world in sin and error pining,
'Till he appeared and the soul felt its worth.
A thrill of hope the weary world rejoices,
For yonder breaks a new and glorious morn;
Fall on your knees, Oh hear the angel voices!
O night divine! O night when Christ was born.
O night, O holy night, O night divine.

Led by the light of Faith serenely beaming;
With glowing hearts by his cradle we stand:
So, led by light of a star sweetly gleaming,
Here come the wise men from Orient land,
The King of Kings lay thus in lowly manger,
In all our trials born to be our friend;
He knows our need, To our weakness no stranger!
Behold your King! Before Him lowly bend!
Behold your King! your King! before him bend!

Truly He taught us to love one another;
His law is Love and His gospel is Peace;
Chains shall he break, for the slave is our brother,
And in his name all oppression shall cease,

Sweet hymns of joy in grateful Chorus raise we;
Let all within us praise his Holy name!
Christ is the Lord, then ever! ever praise we!
His pow'r and glory, evermore proclaim!
His pow'r and glory, evermore proclaim![11]

2. Write a simple prayer for yourself or for others who are on your heart right now.
Think of one or two words for each blank.

God, please help _____.
I long for peace for _____.
Heal _____.
Thank you for _____.

3. Look up.
Following the magi, consider the stars, the sky, the hope we can borrow as we remember our small part in the bigger story.

— When it's dark, go outside if you can; bundle up if you need to.
— Look up; keep your gaze on the stars.
— Open your heart and let yourself feel a little weird, uncomfortable.
— See if you can see some stars. If you can't, imagine them there. Imagine one there. Let the sky speak to you somehow, drawing you in.
— What does it feel like to look up? What can you try to let go of? What does it make you wonder about?

4. To whom can we lend some hope?
In the middle of our pain, sometimes the best thing we can do is help someone. No matter how big or small, a simple kindness can make a big difference to someone else.

Consider:

— Who might need extra love in your circle right now? Is it a friend, family member, coworker, or a group or an organization you care about or whose work you really believe in?
— Offer some tangible encouragement to them—send a card, email, or text; call on the phone; or drop off something they might need.
— Lend some hope.

For Group Reflection

1. Do a last few rounds of sharing in the group, considering these prompts.

Looking back on the four weeks centered on honoring reality, practicing honesty, embracing paradox, and borrowing hope, what are a few highlights you want to hold on to?

- How has processing this material in the group helped you personally?
- What questions of faith has it stirred up in you?
- What actions has it prompted you to consider practicing?

2. Take ten to fifteen minutes to allow each person some contemplative space to use the "Blue Christmas Prayer" prompts below to write their own unique prayer. When you're done, go around the circle and have anyone who's willing share theirs out loud. Depending on the size of the group, you can also combine the responses together into a corporate prayer afterward, including everyone's responses to each line and changing *I* to *we* and *my* to *our*.

A Blue Christmas Prayer

God, this Christmas I am feeling really _____ _____.
I realize I have lost hope in _____.
My faith feels _____.
My mind is _____.
My body is _____.
My soul is _____.
Oh, how I long for _____.
God, I'm trying to let your Love and Hope in, to remember you're in the midst of it all, showing up in small, unexpected ways that are good to notice.

I see you in _____.
I feel you in _____.
I hear you in _____.
I smell you in _____.
I touch you when I touch _____.
Thank you for these gifts.
Despite all the things I can't control, I can still cling to
this: _____.
And for that I am thankful.
God, please keep sustaining me, sustaining us, and illu-
minate what it might mean to rejoice in this weary
world.
Amen.

CHRISTMAS EVE

God with Us

"And they shall name him Emmanuel,"
which means, "God is with us."
—Matthew 1:23b

As sojourners in this weary world, we are in good company with people who are also searching for light when this season is blue. For me, it's helped to honor my own messy grief and the grief of the wider world and respect that the pain we're experiencing is connected to so many others' pain as well. We are not alone. It also reminds me how restorative it is to just be honest and not skip over big feelings or try to make sense of things we truly won't be able to figure out. It is healing to embrace paradoxical realities in the same space at the same time. Yes, it's hard on the soul to do that, but I can borrow hope from others, God, and good data on the resilience of human beings through the ages.

We've also got something that is a precious gift to ponder: *God, who is with us.*

There are three prepositions that can change the way we view living out our faith—*to*, *for*, and *with*. For many of us, we have focused on the prepositions *to* and *for* not just in our life with others—where we do things *to* or *for* people—but also in our relationship with God, where God does things *to* or *for* us.

This theology can really lead down a painful road, especially when we or people in our lives are experiencing tragic loss; sexual, physical, and emotional abuse; chronic or terminal illnesses; mental illness; rejection of our core identity as LGBTQ+; the brutal fall-out of pandemics that sweep through the world; and a long list of other human realities.

A God doing these things *to* us is just . . . cruel.

A God doing these painful things *for* us—for our good, for our growth, for our faith—is just as cruel.

With is a completely different way of living and believing.

Doing *with* others is vulnerable, centered on giving and receiving, where power is diffused and our shared humanity is celebrated.

A God *with us*, in the middle of all of the things I mentioned above, is something I can lean into. God is *with* us in absolutely all of it.

It reminds me of one of the lines in "O Holy Night" that I never noticed until this year:

> The King of Kings lay thus in lowly manger,
> In all our trials born to be our friend.

In all our trials born to be our friend.

As we wrap up our time together and celebrate the eve of Jesus' birth, God-in-the-flesh is on my mind. I love the wild way God chose to enter the world—a human baby born to unlikely parents in the midst of chaos and simplicity. God, born in a smelly stable to an unwed mother and her faithful fiancé. Pagans strangely drawn to him like a moth to a flame. Shepherds, the lowest of the low, getting the news first. God, in the flesh. Showing us the ways of love and how utterly contrary they are to the ways of the world, to the ways of "religion."

"And they shall name him Emmanuel,"
which means, "God is with us." (Matthew 1:23b)

Emmanuel, God is with us.
God is with us.
God, with us.
Some other words for *with* include *accompanying, alongside, amid, among, beside, by, for, including, near, upon, as companion, side by side, in the thick of.*

All these words are good for my weary heart, for our weary world.

God accompanying us. God alongside us. God amid us. God among us. God beside us. God by us. God including us. God near us. God plus us. God upon us. God as companion to us. God side by side us. God in the thick of us (that's my personal favorite).

God, in the thick of us—in the thick of our humanity, our pain, our blue, our beautiful, our hard, our messy, our ugly, our struggles, our joys.

God, in the middle of this weary world, with us.

As God is with us, we are also called to be in-the-flesh with others in the muck and mire of their real lives, too. Accompanying others. Alongside others. Amid others. Beside others. By others. For others. Including others. Near others. A companion to others. Side by side with others. In the thick of others.

God, with us. In the thick of our messy, beautiful lives.

Us, with others. In the thick of their messy, beautiful lives.

God, with the world. In the thick of its messy, beautiful existence.

In that, a weary world rejoices.

Maybe our weary hearts can, too.

FOR FAMILY
AND FRIENDS

What Helps,
What Hurts

"I'm not perfect and I am not always right, but I'm here,
open, paying attention, loving you, and fully engaged."
— Brené Brown[1]

It says a lot about your heart that you're reading *A Weary World* and considering how you can be a better companion to a friend, family member, or coworker who's extra weary this season and struggling with Christmas. It is meaningful that you care and can still hold your joy while also allowing room for others who are in different places. Here are a few possibilities to consider as you travel alongside folks who feel differently than you—what sometimes hurts and what might help. Each person is unique, so remember that what I share here is only a launching point. The best thing you can always center on is being a person of presence, just being with others without answers, judgment, or perceived solutions. Being direct and open is usually appreciated (and often rare), and these three simple questions offer a good place to start:

How can I be a good friend to you during this season?
What helps you or brings a little relief?
What hurts you?

A lot of us don't know what we *need* when we're hurting, but a lot of times we know what offers a little relief and what causes more pain.

Below are some broad strokes on what hurts and what helps — for all of us to ponder.

What Hurts

Spiritual platitudes. Spiritual platitudes are phrases that often get thrown out there to feel like we are offering up some hope or peace, but for the most part they just don't help most people. It's fair to think them all you want in your own head, but to really be a supporter of people experiencing grief and loss during this season, consider keeping them to yourself. Saying, "God loves you," "I'll pray for you to feel better," "Have you tried _____?," "God has a plan," or passing on unsolicited Scripture verses really don't help anyone feel more connected; rather, such actions contribute to the disconnection we are feeling and can make us feel like projects or somehow less than.

Trying to cajole us out of our feelings. Learning to sit with people's honest feelings and not fix, give advice, scripturize, minimize, or cajole people into feeling differently is an art and takes a lot of practice. Hold back from trying to move beyond just honoring the feelings the person is expressing. Stop yourself from adding anything to their experience other than "I hear you," "I feel you," "I see you," "I'm with you." I'll say it again: *I hear you, I feel you, I see you, I'm with you.*

Expectations. When we are struggling with grief and pain in different ways, the last thing we need is pressure or expectations we know we will not be able to meet. It's hard when you want someone to be happier than they are, to not be suffering so much, or to do what you think they need to or *should* do. One of the most harmful things is laying on overt or covert guilt and expectations that make people feel more burdened than they already are.

Judgment. Often, we have our own measures of what's right and wrong, good or bad, godly or worldly. It is extremely painful to pass on these judgments to people hurting during this season, judging what we deem is acceptable by our measures, our standards, and our experiences. People who are struggling are likely already harshly judging themselves; they don't need any extra judgment to manage.

Withdrawing. Sometimes friends and family members can feel so cautious about saying the wrong thing that we do what's simplest—withdraw under the guise of "giving someone space." It's fine if space is what people say will help, but most of the time, withdrawing out of fear ends up leaving people who are struggling more isolated, disconnected, and lonely. There's a fine line, but no communication usually always hurts.

What Helps

Listening ears. One of the greatest gifts we can give each other when Christmas is blue is a listening ear and presence without judgment. Practicing the principle of "more ears, less mouth"[2] doesn't come easy for some of us, but it's so helpful to those of us who are grieving, struggling, crawling, or wrestling with God, ourselves, or others.

Let us be right where we are. This means not trying to get us to where you think we should be or back to where we were. It's trusting us and God over the long story and honoring our current feelings. It's hard to hold hurt, pain, grief, and angst, but it really does help when people let us be where we're at without judgment.

Give us freedom. The holiday season comes with countless expectations, parties, events, family gatherings, and things that can feel extremely stressful for so many. Giving freedom for people to say, "Yes," "No," or "I changed my mind and can't come" (without holding it against us) is so helpful. This kind of grace is greatly needed when Christmas is blue.

Stay in the present. It's easy to want to move people to the future—to get them to where they feel and are doing better, but being willing to sit with us in the dark in the here and now is what most of us desperately need.

Unconditional love. One of the most tender and beautiful gifts we can receive when we're struggling is unconditional love. The experience of feeling that no matter where we're at, no matter what we believe, no matter what we're doing or not doing, no matter how badly we're struggling, no matter how much we're wrestling, to know we are still deeply and unconditionally loved by people in our lives is everything.

Your willingness to be a kind presence in a harsh season matters! Lastly, I encourage you to be gentle with yourself; you will not be able to hit everything right or escape feeling like you might be walking on eggshells. It's very likely you'll make mistakes and hang up the phone and wish you hadn't said this or that. Remember, none of this is science. Journeying alongside people in the muck and mire of real life is an art. Be creative, be true to yourself, and hold on to the most important thing you can offer someone who is hurting—long-haul unconditional love and presence.

For Ministry Leaders

Caring for People Experiencing a Blue Christmas

It's the most wonderful time of the year.
— Eddie Pola / George Wyle[1]

"It's the most wonderful time of the year" . . . until it's not.

First of all, thank you for your willingness to integrate options for people in your congregations, teams, and groups who may be wrestling with less-than-merry feelings this season. It's important to recognize that no matter what's being expressed on the surface, so many people silently struggle during the Advent season, afraid to share the truth in certain contexts for fear of being fixed, scripturized, shamed, or judged. Others may be subtly or overtly oozing pain all over the place, and you're not quite sure what to do about it. Many others are just trudging through the holidays, going through the motions while their souls are weary, literally counting down the days until they're over. This material can't cover the wide range of hurt and struggle that people are experiencing this time of year, but hopefully it's a solid resource for you and your teams to consider.

There are some things you can, indeed, do as leaders to help create a safer and braver space for the wider ranges of experiences people are going through this time of year. Below are several primary principles to consider trying in your communities. Of course, feel free to adapt anything to your context, language, group, or theological persuasions.

Acknowledge the wide range of feelings in every room, every church service, every place where people are gathered this season. Some are feeling close to God, others far away; some excited and engaged about Christmas, and some feeling like they want to run away; some suffering deep grief from recent loss, and others being triggered for a myriad of reasons. Trauma is real; it's in every group year-round, but a lot of it surfaces more evidently during this season. It's important for faith communities—places where people are coming in search of hope and connection for their real lives—to help bring it to the surface for not only individuals but for the health of the entire group.

Beware of Christian platitudes. A lot of spiritual phrases roll off a lot of our tongues readily and do far more harm than we realize. Avoid statements like, "God says . . . ," "Yes, but have you tried . . . ?," "Jesus loves you," and peppering people with Scriptures that you think they might really need to hear. Many people have heard these things for a long time and are longing to be heard, understood, and held—not preached to. Much better alternatives: "Tell me more"; "I'm with you"; "It's really hard."

Give people freedom. Remind others, "If you need to, feel free to step out of conversations that are too intense for you." "Take good care of yourselves; stay for what you can and leave when you need to." "This is what we'll be doing at this gathering, and it's okay if it's not something that will be good for you right now." This simple reminder can help some of us breathe a little easier and help remind us of our agency and ability to make choices we need for our own mental health.

Be careful about assumptions. It's easy to assume everyone has family to connect with, children who are excited about Christmas, money to buy presents, or too much to eat during the holidays; we often toss these things into our sermons and communication without realizing how many people are silently struggling. These are privileged middle-class assumptions often embedded into our language and culture that cause shame and disconnection; they can be very harmful to abuse victims, people struggling with infertility, orphans, single parents and struggling families, and people who might look like they're staying afloat but are actually sinking and no one knows.

Create contemplative spaces for people to share grief, loss, and pain. Every community is different, but any opportunities for people to feel heard and have a space to express themselves is usually helpful. Maybe it's a prayer station with candles, a place to write cries of the heart, a reflective space for journaling or art. Blue Christmas gatherings are possibilities, but it's crucial to remember the season lasts for a while. It's helpful to weave possibilities throughout the month and not only rely on one event. At The Refuge, we have a chalkboard partition that we often use for people to write or draw reflections or responses to a contemplative question.

Share resources with your community. If you aren't hosting a Blue Christmas gathering, find out what other churches are. Where are there other opportunities for honesty, care, and healing—support groups and other community gatherings that could be helpful to your folks? What other local mental and spiritual health resources are available to people? Consider how you can help make them more accessible for people, maybe by sharing the information, partnering with local nonprofits, offering transportation, or assisting with any fees. Offer suicide prevention training openly, making conversations about mental health and depression during the holidays more normal.

Notice what's going on for yourself and get the support you need. The holiday season from Advent through Christmas Eve and the start of the new year are extremely taxing for pastors and ministry leaders. The busyness takes an extra toll on the helpers. Make sure you're taking good care of yourself, getting the space and support you need to stay healthy.

Blue Christmas
Resources

These days, more and more churches and communities are offering Blue Christmas services and gatherings. Years ago, when The Refuge held space this way for the first time, our founder of Blue Christmas, Jennifer Herrick—an incredible artist and contemplative activist—pulled together things from scratch because there were so few options. Now there are countless possibilities to draw from, and if you search online for "Blue Christmas resources and ideas," you will get a wide range of possibilities to consider. Below are some creative ideas and themes to explore as well as a list of books and sites to check out. Any of these can be adapted for the online environment, too. (See www.wjkbooks.com/AWearyWorld for some digital resources.)

Liturgical Elements

A wide range of liturgies for Blue Christmas are available based on different denominational affiliations, traditions, and church cultures. For some, including a lot of Scripture will be healing, while for others it may not provide as much comfort as inspiration from other kinds of literature. Some communities like to gather corporately with printed liturgies with reader-responses, and others might only do self-guided contemplative stations with no specific group time. If you do gather as a group for at least part of your experience, below are a few possible passages you might want to draw from and a few other liturgical ideas to consider.

- *Scriptures:* Psalm 23; Psalm 40; Psalm 139; Matthew 5:3–10
- *Silence:* A space for silence to consider, ground, and reflect.
- *Music:* There are so many possibilities for music, and each community is different, but consider meaningful songs for listening and reflection. I would suggest using corporate singing sparingly for Blue Christmas gatherings because suggesting that "we should sing" can inspire a lot of conflicting feelings instead of comfort.
- *Simple responses:* Build prayer responses that are as inclusive as possible and stay away from forced gratitude or belief. Consider phrases like, "We ache," "We cry out to you," "We weep," "We wait," "We long for . . . ."
- *Lectio Divina*: Read Scripture, poetry, or other pieces of literature multiple times, allowing people to notice words or phrases that resonate and consider what emotions they might evoke.
- *Visio Divina (sacred seeing)*: Display art for people to reflect on and notice: What emotions do these images evoke? What questions might the images bring forth? What prayer might they inspire?
- *A space for feeling words to be shared:* Ask people to offer one-word responses to how they're feeling or what they are experiencing this season.

Candle Lightings

Light seems to be really healing in this season of darkness. Consider using candles in different ways. There are countless ideas, but below are a few possibilities:

— A prayer altar for people to light candles and offer prayers.
— Make candles available for people to take home and draw strength from during the month.
— As a liturgy, consider a guided candle lighting with four separate candles for different losses and experiences.

Candle 1: Those who have died this year.
Possible wording: *We light this first candle to remember the people in our lives who died this past year, whose presence we ache for, whose spirit we are missing, whose absence we grieve.* Response: *God, we ache.*

Candle 2: Honoring the pain of other losses—people, relationships, health, jobs, faith, dreams.
Possible wording: *This light represents the wide range of losses we and others in our lives are grieving right now—broken relationships, the loss of health, jobs, faith that used to be certain, and dreams that were shattered.* Response: *God, we're grieving.*

Candle 3: To honor ourselves, our souls, what we're feeling and experiencing.
Possible wording: *We light this candle for our weary souls, for the burdens we are carrying, for our heavy hearts.* Response: *God, we long for light.*

Candle 4: A desire for hope and peace.
Possible wording: *We light this candle as a symbol of our desire for hope and peace in this season, to remember that despite the darkness, light and love can seep in.* Response: *God, we're open.*

Reflection Stations

Creating contemplative spaces to open up minds, hearts, and souls can be extremely healing, especially in a season of a lot of words. Making interactive stations where people can engage at their own pace, in their own way, can often be healing. As you're creating them for your unique contexts, consider building in tangible, experiential forms of expression—creating art, breaking stuff, tactile examples, writing prompts, bodily movement, community art pieces, burning paper, working with Play-Doh, crafting symbols and icons.

Some possible themes and creative ideas to consider and adapt are as follows:

Grief and Loss
  — Collecting "tears" in a bottle, incorporating Psalm 56:8 with small bottles of water to take home.
  — Writing losses on strips of paper and tying them to stark branches.
  — Using tongs or protective gloves, placing broken pieces of glass in a jar to take home.

Fear
  — Breathing prayer station: Breathe in _____, Breathe out _____, or a phrase on the in-breath and a different one on the out-breath. (See examples on page 27–28.)
  — A large mirror on which to write different things we fear.
  — Making collages with words or images.

Anger
  — Ornament smashing station, ensuring safety with sufficient space and protective gear.
  — Writing angry feelings on strips of paper and ripping them up into smaller bits of paper.
  — Expressing anger through words or images on office copier or notebook paper and putting the paper through a shredder.
  — Pounding station with thick wooden boards, large nails, and hammers.

Emotional Pain
  — Build your own wailing wall—a place where people can write prayers and place them in the cracks.
  — Write painful messages or hurts on bandages or use bandages for a quiet reflection.

Spiritual Doubts and Questions
  — Write questions about God and faith on a large chalkboard or whiteboard.
  — Decorate paper stars with reflections on the vastness of God's universe.
  — God out of the box: How are we expanding our image of God?

Family Wounds
  — "Baggage" station with suitcases or backpacks and bricks or rocks to write on that represent things we're trying to unload. These items can be moved out of their container and placed near a cross or in a pile to symbolize release and healing.
  — Writing cards to oneself with loving messages or replacing negative messages with more compassionate ones: *You are loved. You are not alone. You are valuable. You are enough. I am with you.*
  — Draw a family on a chalkboard and have people write words or draw images that reflect feelings about our family.

Forgiveness
  — Utilize water, dropping rocks into water to release unforgiveness or writing on dissolving paper.
  — Special Communion station focused on forgiving others, ourselves, even God.

Peace
  — Blankets or textiles to bring comfort.
  — Stress balls or other tools for relief.

— Meditative music station—a place to listen with headphones.
— Guided meditation station.

Celebrating the Good
— Honoring small gifts in our lives using wrapping paper or boxes.
— Creating a community art piece in collage or paint that symbolizes growth, transformation, or what's good right now.

Caring for Neighbors
— List local needs to consider, with prompts to ask God to show us who we might need to reach out to; partner organizations could also be featured.
— Consider a focus on immigration (perfect for the Christmas story), racism, classism, sexism, ableism, and other areas people are passionate about and need to process.

Other Resources to Read or Access

— *Blue Christmas Online*, at bluechristmasonline.com. This site is hosted by The Refuge, my faith community, with all of the liturgies, reflection stations, and other resources we've used over many years of facilitating Blue Christmas as well as a list of other resources to access.
— My friend Christine Sine is an author, contemplative, and curator of liturgies and prayers. She has countless prayers for Advent and Blue Christmas that are easily accessible, beautiful, and healing at Godspacelight.com.
— Jan Richardson's books *The Cure for Sorrow: A Book of Blessings for Times of Grief* and *Circle of Grace: A Book of Blessings for the Seasons* are excellent resources. She

also offers an online Advent group during the season at janrichardson.com.

— *The Work of the People* at theworkofthepeople.com. There are numerous videos, visual liturgies, and other resources you can pay to download that are raw and real and are made for group and church use.

— Megan Devine's book *It's OK That You're Not OK* is an excellent resource for grief, and refugeingrief. com has a wide range of resources to draw from for a better understanding of grief and loss.

What are some other resources you've found? Share them with me at kathyaescobar@gmail.com so that they can be added to the bluechristmasonline.com resource list.

Notes

Introduction

1. Parker J. Palmer, *A Hidden Wholeness* (San Francisco: Jossey Bass, 2004), 126.

2. Adolphe-Charles Adam and Placide Cappeau, "O Holy Night," trans., John Sullivan Dwight, Esq., The Hymns and Carols of Christmas, https://www.hymnsandcarolsofchristmas.com/Hymns_and _Carols/o_holy_night.htm, accessed February 1, 2020, adapted.

Week One: Honoring Reality

1. Henri J. M. Nouwen, *Life of the Beloved* (New York: Crossroad, 1992), 87.

2. Nouwen, *Life of the Beloved*, 87.

3. Francis Weller and Rashani Rea, *The Threshold between Loss and Revelation* (n.p.: Sacred Spiral Press, 2017).

4. Mirabai Starr, *Wild Mercy* (Louisville, CO: Sounds True, 2019), 137.

5. Ruth Hogan, *The Keeper of Lost Things: A Novel* (New York: HarperCollins, 2017), 59.

6. John Lennon and Paul McCartney, "Let It Be," https://www .lyrics.com/lyric/4372823/, accessed December 24, 2020.

7. Refuge in Grief, https://www.refugeingrief.com, accessed February 15, 2020.

8. Barbara Taylor Brown, *Learning to Walk in the Dark* (New York: HarperCollins, 2014), 5.

9. Pema Chodron, *When Things Fall Apart: Heart Advice for Difficult Times* (Boulder, CO: Shambhala, 2013), 144.

10. Anne Lamott, "My Mind Is a Bad Neighborhood I Try Not to Go into Alone," *Salon*, March 13, 1997, https://www.salon.com/1997/03/13/lamott970313/.

11. Kathy Escobar, *Practicing: Changing Yourself to Change the World* (Louisville, KY: Westminster John Knox Press, 2020), 8–9.

Week Two: Practicing Honesty

1. Karla McLaren, *Emotional Genius* (promotional copy, Sounds True, 2002), https://www.learnoutloud.com/Catalog/Self-Development/Emotional-Development/Emotional-Genius/15955, accessed March 9, 2020.

2. Kathy Escobar, *Practicing: Changing Yourself to Change the World* (Louisville, KY: Westminster John Knox Press, 2020), 1.

3. Harriet Lerner, *The Dance of Anger* (New York: Harper and Row, 1985), 1.

4. Jan Richardson, *The Cure for Sorrow: A Book of Blessings for Times of Grief* (Orlando, FL: Wanton Gospeller Press, 2016), 50.

5. Richardson, *The Cure for Sorrow*, xvii.

6. Jen Sincero, *You Are a Badass: How to Stop Doubting Your Greatness and Start Living an Awesome Life* (Philadelphia: Running Press, 2013), 168.

7. Brené Brown, *Daring Greatly: How the Courage to Be Vulnerable Transforms the Way We Live, Love, Parent and Lead* (New York: Penguin, 2012), 75.

8. Brené Brown, *The Gifts of Imperfection* (Center City, MN: Hazelden, 2010), 41.

9. Brown, *Daring Greatly*, 75.

10. Jamie Arpin-Ricci, *Vulnerable Faith: Missional Living in the Radical Way of St. Patrick* (Brewster, MA: Paraclete, 2013), 166.

11. Melody Beattie, *Codependent No More: How to Stop Controlling Others and Start Caring for Yourself* (Center City, MN: Hazelden, 1986), 146.

12. Marshall Rosenberg, *Nonviolent Communication: A Language of Life* (Encinitas, CA: PuddleDancer Press, 2015).

Week Three: Embracing Paradox

1. Leonard Cohen, "Anthem," https://www.lyrics.com/lyric/1638490/Leonard+Cohen/Anthem, accessed March 1, 2020.

2. Henry Cloud, *Changes That Heal: How to Understand Your Past to Ensure a Healthier Future* (Grand Rapids: Zondervan, 1990), chap. 12.

3. Richard Rohr, *The Naked Now: Learning to See as the Mystics See* (New York: Crossroad, 2009), 132.

4. Mirabai Starr, *Wild Mercy* (Louisville, CO: Sounds True, 2019), 49.

5. Starr, *Wild Mercy*, 49.

6. J. R. R. Tolkien, *The Lord of the Rings: One Volume* (New York: Houghton Mifflin, 2005), 348.

7. Tolkien, *The Lord of the Rings*, 348.

8. Jason Mraz, "The Beauty in Ugly," https://www.azlyrics.com/lyrics/jasonmraz/thebeautyinugly.html, accessed March 8, 2020.

9. Anne Lamott, *Plan B: Further Thoughts on Faith* (New York: Penguin, 2005), 275.

10. Parker J. Palmer, *A Hidden Wholeness* (San Francisco: Jossey Bass, 2004), 91–92.

11. Brennan Manning, *The Ragamuffin Gospel* (Sisters, OR: Multnomah, 2003), 23.

12. Coleman Barks, trans., *The Rumi Book of Love: Poems of Ecstasy and Longing* (New York: HarperCollins, 2003), 109.

Week Four: Borrowing Hope

1. Bryan Stevenson, *Just Mercy: A Story of Justice and Redemption* (New York: Random House), 241.

2. Thomas Merton, *The Seven Storey Mountain* (New York: Harcourt Press, 1944), 208.

3. Adolphe-Charles Adam and Placide Cappeau, "O Holy Night," https://www.hymnsandcarolsofchristmas.com/Hymns_and_Carols/o_holy_night.htm, accessed February 1, 2020, adapted.

4. Maya Angelou, "Still I Rise," https://poets.org/poem/still-i-rise, accessed April 25, 2020.

5. Brené Brown, *Rising Strong: The Reckoning, The Rumble, The Revolution* (New York: Penguin Random House, 2015), chap. 1. Kindle.

6. Heatherlyn, "Be Here Now," https://heatherlynmusic.band camp.com/track/be-here-now-2.

7. Heatherlyn, "Be Here Now."

8. Adam and Cappeau, "O Holy Night."

9. Mary Oliver, *Red Bird* (Boston: Beacon, 2009), 104.

10. Oliver, *Red Bird*, 105.

11. Adam and Cappeau, "O Holy Night."

For Family and Friends

1. Brené Brown, *Daring Greatly: How the Courage to Be Vulnerable Transforms the Way We Live, Love, Parent and Lead* (New York: Penguin, 2012), 237.

2. Kathy Escobar, *Practicing: Changing Yourself to Change the World* (Louisville, KY: Westminster John Knox Press, 2020), 35.

For Ministry Leaders

1. Eddie Pola and George Wyle, "It's the Most Wonderful Time of the Year," https://www.lyrics.com/lyric/31579931/It%27s+the+Most +Wonderful+Time+of+the+Year, accessed April 26, 2020.

ALSO BY KATHY ESCOBAR

FAITH IS A VERB
MEANT TO BE PRACTICED

"The world has never been in more need of a book like this."
—JOHN PAVLOVITZ, author of *A Bigger Table*

Practicing

CHANGING YOURSELF
TO CHANGE THE WORLD

KATHY ESCOBAR

9780664265847 • $18.00

"*Practicing* is both deeply moving and incredibly insightful. I know it will be both a place of refuge and a catalyst for transformation for those fortunate enough to read it. The world has never been more in need of a book like this."

—JOHN PAVLOVITZ,
author of *A Bigger Table*

You have more power to change the world than you realize, and it starts with practice. Featuring ten transformational practices, *Practicing* is for those who want to live out their faith through real action. Practices include healing, equalizing, advocating, and more. Perfect for group or individual study!

WJK WESTMINSTER JOHN KNOX PRESS

1.800.523.1631 • www.wjkbooks.com

CPSIA information can be obtained
at www.ICGtesting.com
Printed in the USA
JSHW041027031020
8492JS00007B/144

9 780664 266936